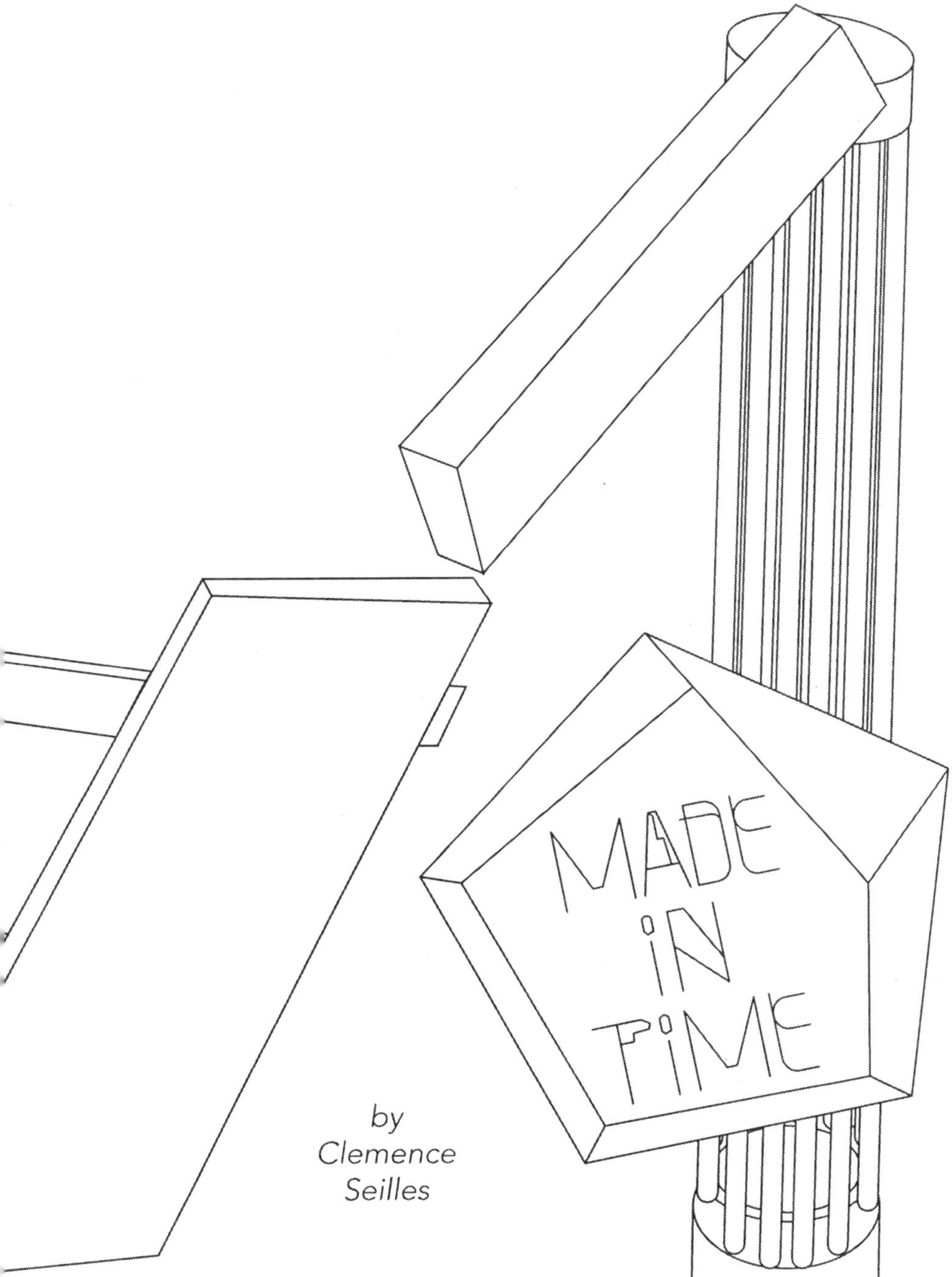

by
Clemence
Seilles

1

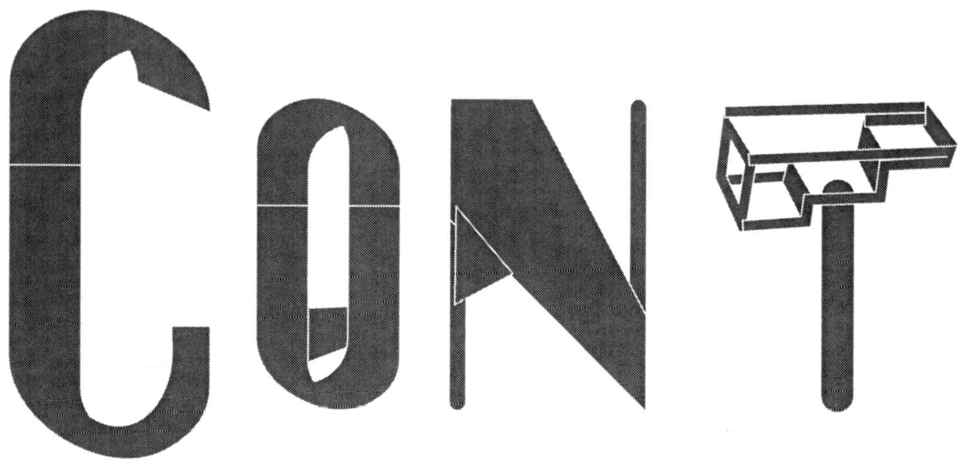

THANK YOU

To Sarah Gottlieb and George Wu at Household, who have worked with me on this book. To all the people that in different ways have supported this project.

'We need to fall down the stairs'.

Display Type: T.O.D, designed by Sarah Gottlieb and George Wu 2008. Inspired by Clemence Seilles' project Made in Time. Each letter was designed in randomely chosen time slots, from 1 - 8 minutes, using the ready made forms taken from Seilles' drawings.
www.house-hold.org

Body Text: Avenir was designed in 1988 by Adrian Frutiger. Avenir is French for Future and the typeface takes inspiration from early geometric sans-serif typefaces Erbar and Futura. Frutiger intended Avenir to be a more organic, humanist interpretation of these highly geometric types.

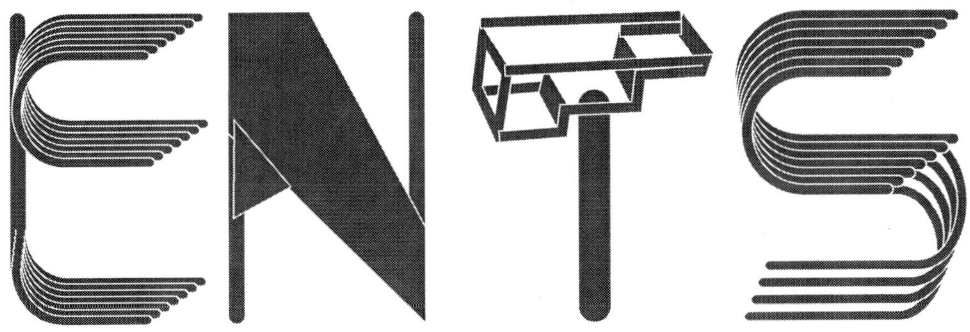

BERLIN LETTERS

Built in a specific time frame for a specified period with a unique function on a unique place. It would be a rather long and complicated description you could give for the installations Clemence has built in these last months. Her research focuses on very personal design, design that is made for one defined user for one specific goal.

She has created several installations, including a bookshop for Koening Books at Royal College of Art. This work was created within the context of the Royal College of Art. Another project comprises of a bed/ sleeping unit, made for a friend within the context of her room. He came to London for 5 weeks, and needed a place to sleep during this time. Instead of putting a mattress on the floor Clemence created a micro world in her room for her guest. She didn't want him to take up too much space. The low bed is about 60 cm width. Connected to the bed, about 50 cm above from where he would lie is a wooden construction with beams, like a hat-rack, where clothes and other luggage can be stored. The complete space the guest would take up within the 5 weeks has been to an absolute minimum.

All works, as she noted very precisely in the subject of the email with images she sent, are made within a specific time frame, and can or should be used in a specified time period. he always makes the work by herself, using wood and tape, a very hand crafted way of working and going into the work. I see Clemence working with various tools. I see her working in an overall on her new benches. There is always a beautiful emphasis on the hand-crafted part of her work.

The very strict time schedule reminds me of two things. On the one hand, I imagine a constructor who makes appointments and deals with the people he works for: The kitchen should be installed in two weeks. But this frame doesn't matter for the object itself, since it will last for years and years, and actually later in the process it wouldn't matter if a constructor had spent 10 or 7 days building the kitchen, since that will be long forgotten when you can cook with new equipment.

More than working like a constructor, the time schedules Clemence works with seem to me to be silent performances of some sort. The whole creative process, from drawing to production, takes place in one single space. It reminds me of the piece she did a year ago, Made in Time, recently re-enacted a few weeks ago. People could bet how long it would take to make various pieces of work. In this performance the betting was also a part of the project, but what in general makes these ticking clocks so important for her objects?

This emphasis on the building process, the period of time it takes to make the work and using her own hands to build and create it, makes Clemence's projects all the more worthy. The very personal designs Clemence aims to produce are also in the whole time schedule. For things that were made in a factory, where 1500 cups are made per minute, or 13 parts of a bed per minute, the length of time a machine has worked on the objects are irrelevant. It might amaze people how fast you can make 1500 cups, but this amazement will not lead to more appreciation of the object itself. It is about a fascination for machinery. Clemence's objects of design are actually hand made, and exclusively produced for a certain time frame and for a certain use. This leads to a new way of thinking about objects. Wouldn't they seem more important to us if we would knew how much time was spent on them? Yes indeed.

And now to come back to the idea of a performance. To me the act of building and setting a time schedule for particular projects, creates performances with results that are actually visible. The objects do not only act as documentation of the performance, but they are the result and the main goal of the act of building. I really like the idea that the performance – if it is meant this way – is in the end as important as the object itself; the building process and the object created are completely equal to each other.

Temporary

Just a few days ago Clemence emailed me about the office space, where she is going to build a sleeping and living unit within two weeks to live in. Taking this former commercial space as a starting point for building something seems interesting. She takes the work out of the context of the Royal College of Art, and out of the home context. Entering this non-space, a space yet without meaning, and with only a former context.

The sense of temporality and empty spaces brings me to write about Berlin. A few weeks ago walking in Berlin I came across one of these spaces in the city. Just a block away from a lively street, there was a hole in the city. The empty spot was of course created by the Berlin Wall. Around the Wall there would always be an emptiness of about 1 or 2 kilometers, where houses have disappeared or where people have left their homes. Now, almost 10 years after the break down of the wall, the spots are disappearing more and more. Berlin is becoming busier and larger, expanding within the known borders.

Two years ago there seemed more space. The Berlin Biennale used an empty building in the August-strasse just across Kunstwerke, as its headquarters. A former ground school for Jewish girls which hadn't been used for over 10 years. WithIn the abandoned building: classrooms, gyms and corridors were used to install art. It was a really powerful presentation, using this empty space for art, the former context slumbering somewhere in the background, yet sometimes so physically present.

Since then the Berlin Biennale has attracted more and more people who now are happy to occupy the empty lots. They move from one empty district to the another, until the area is occupied again by tourists etc. So Clemence, don't wait too long before going there. I'm looking forward to seeing you building there.

MADE IN A YEAR

The drawings, photographs, objects, and writings found in this publication were all produced within a year at the Royal College of Art, with the help of the generous assistance from people who led my insecure steps. This book, which is again the result of a partnership turned into friendship, attempts to relate the entire process I have undertaken this last year. The aim was to define the character I want to be as a Product Designer, an area to work on, a way to work with my own techniques, medium, tools…

Time has gone so fast this year, and it has always pushed me to accomplish what I wanted. Working and living under time pressure. I don't mean that I have been creating situations of uneasiness and discomfort for myself and others (not on purpose, at least). What I actually like is to consider that everything has an end, and it is by confronting the inevitable end of an experience that I can feel things are existing. They exist even more because I know that they will disappear, or be transformed, moved to another stage. This is almost literally what I intended to translate into the objects and spaces that I have constructed: a temporary stage.

May 2008

MARKS ON PAPER

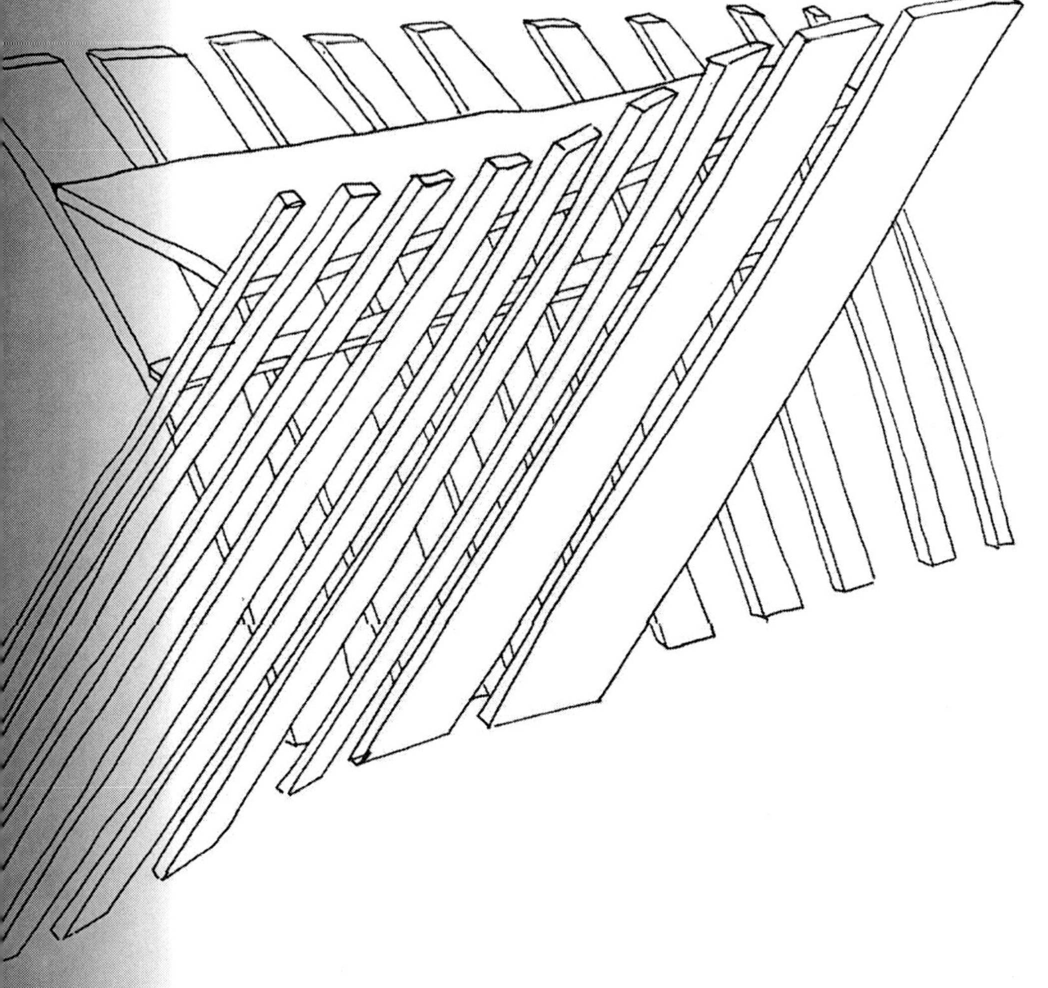

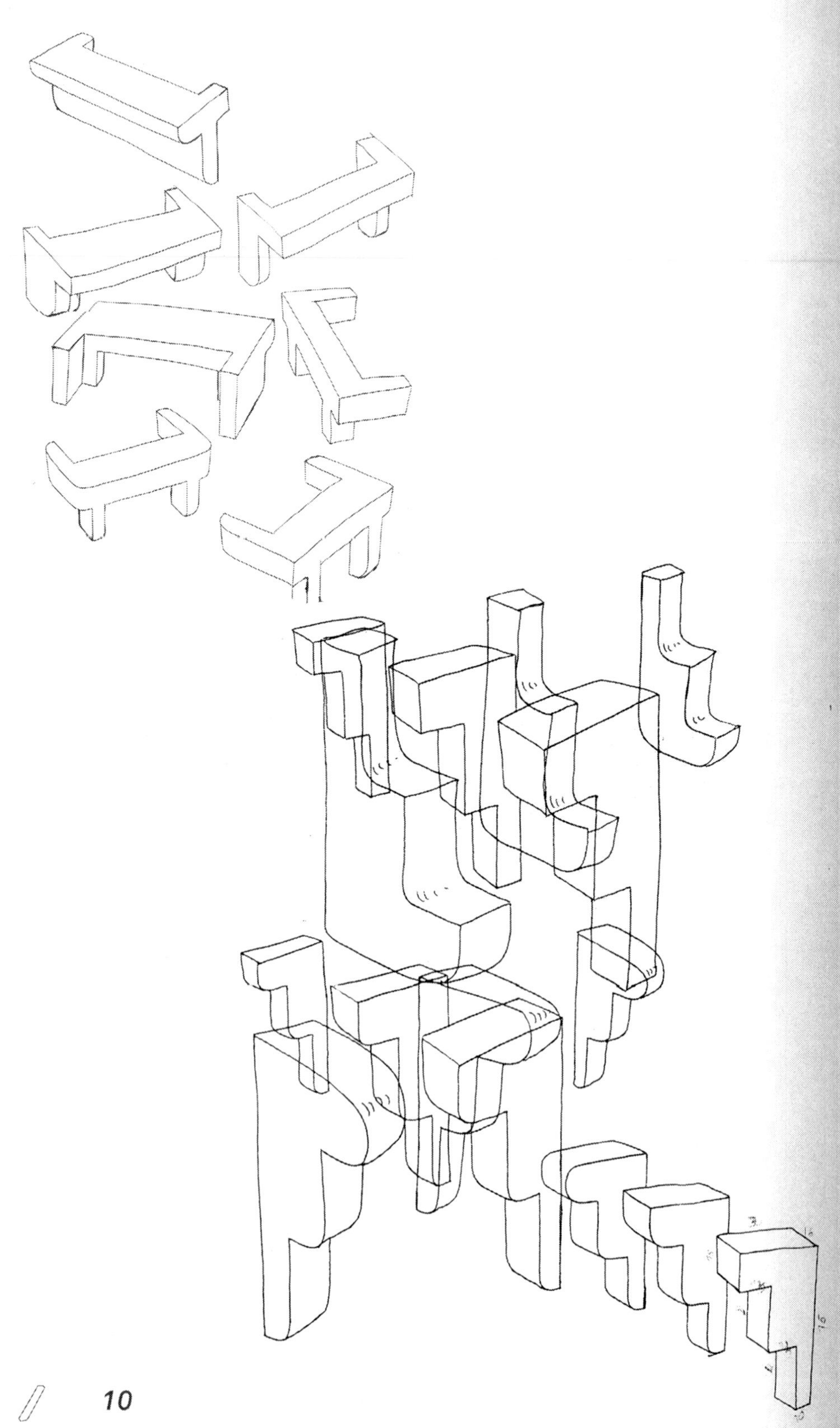

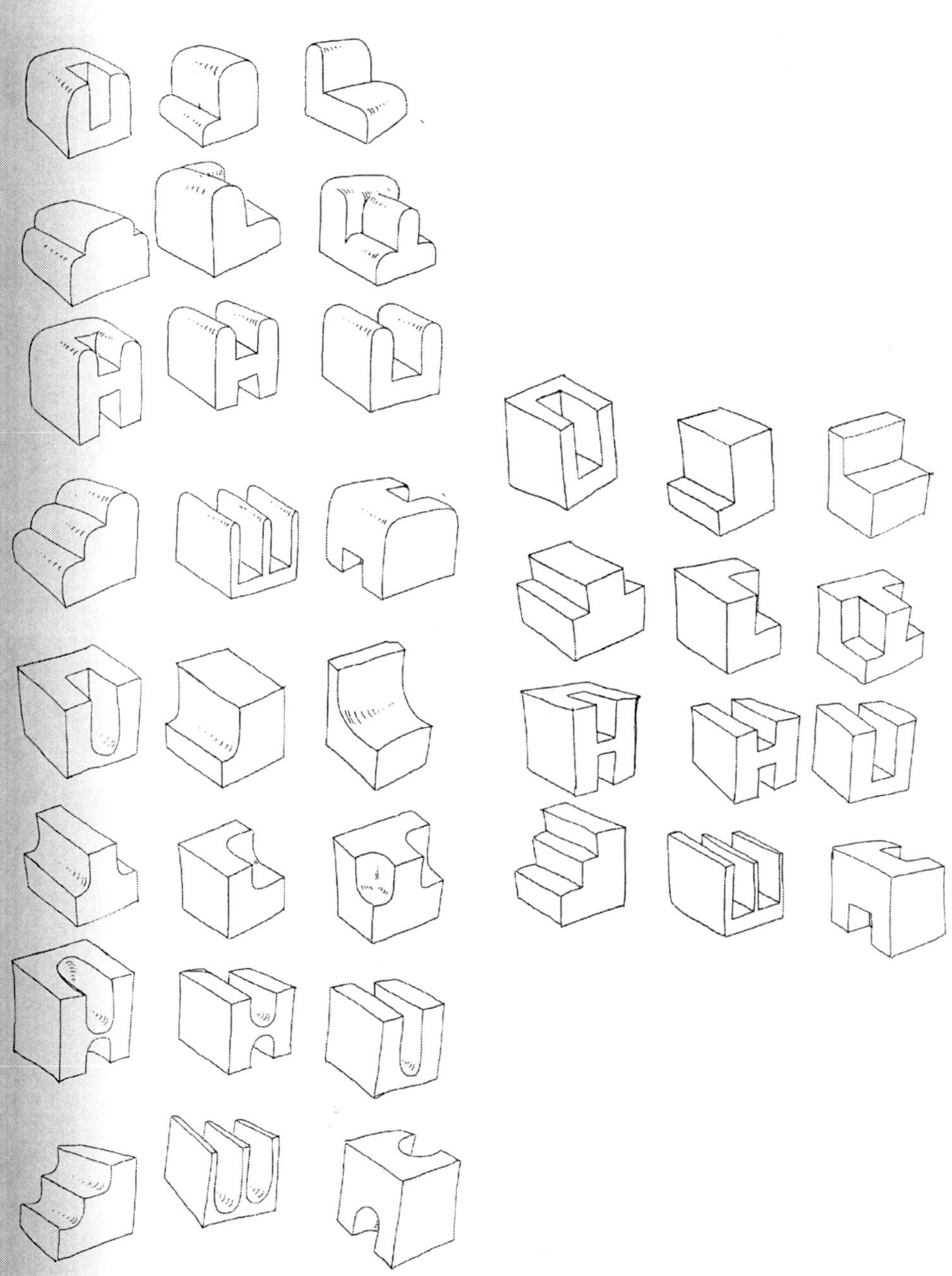

MARKS ON PAPER

In that closet I keep innumerable pencils, colored pencils too, and a box of pencils in 90 different colors, a big black English box that Michele gave me. There are temperas, watercolor boxes, brushes, inks, rubbers, pencil sharpeners, fixatives and a variety of glues. When I open the doors of that closet an inebriating smell comes out of it, a faintly chemical, vaguely exotic smell, an affectionate smell.

Perhaps my desire to do drawings comes out of that closet, along with those mysterious odors or maybe the drawings start from the desire to leave marks on those white sheets of paper, with those pencils and those soft colors.

I don't think there are any more urgent functionalities than these, which prompt me to do drawings.

Ettore Sottsass. Published in Terrazzo, n. 4, Milan, Spring 1990.

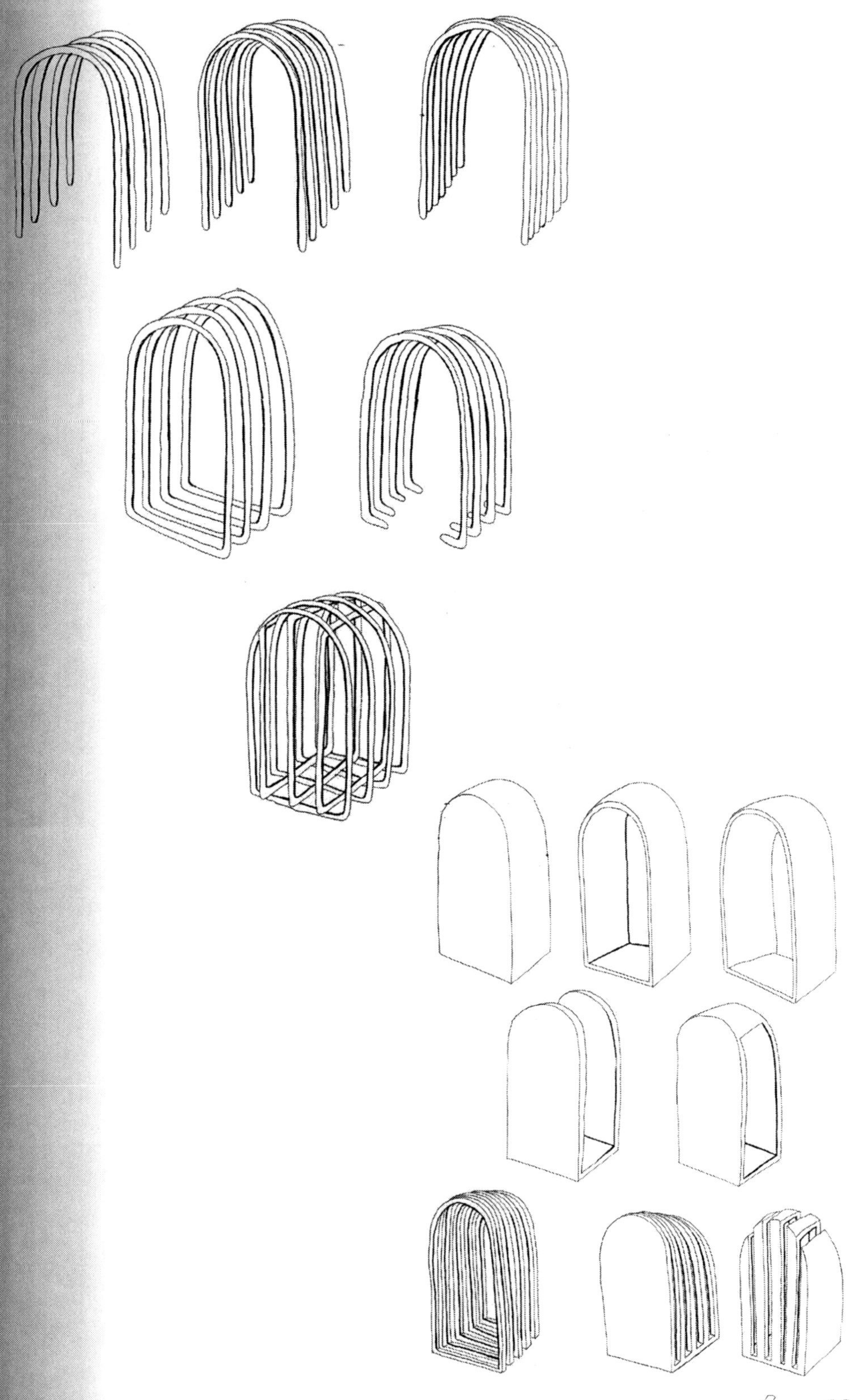

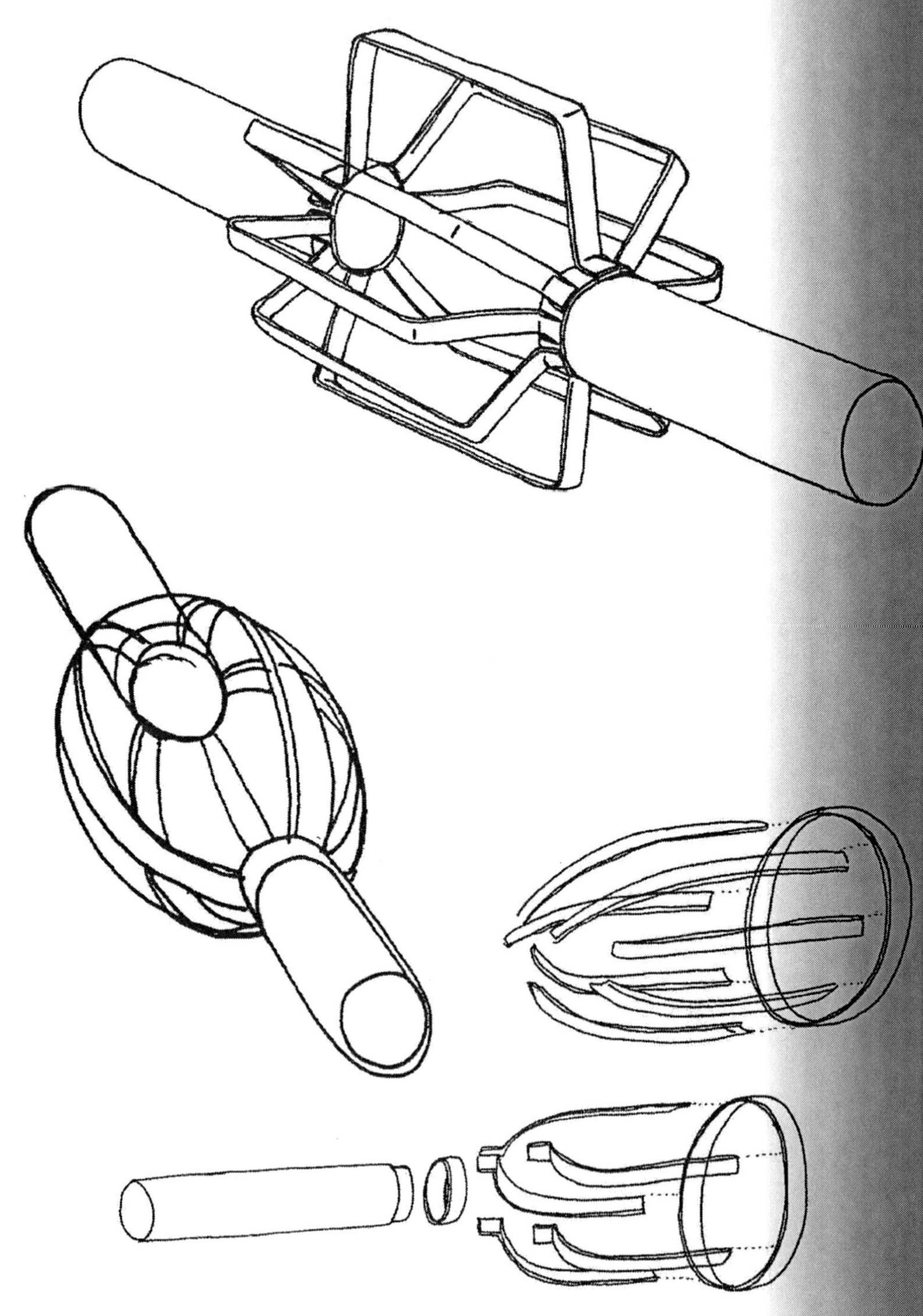

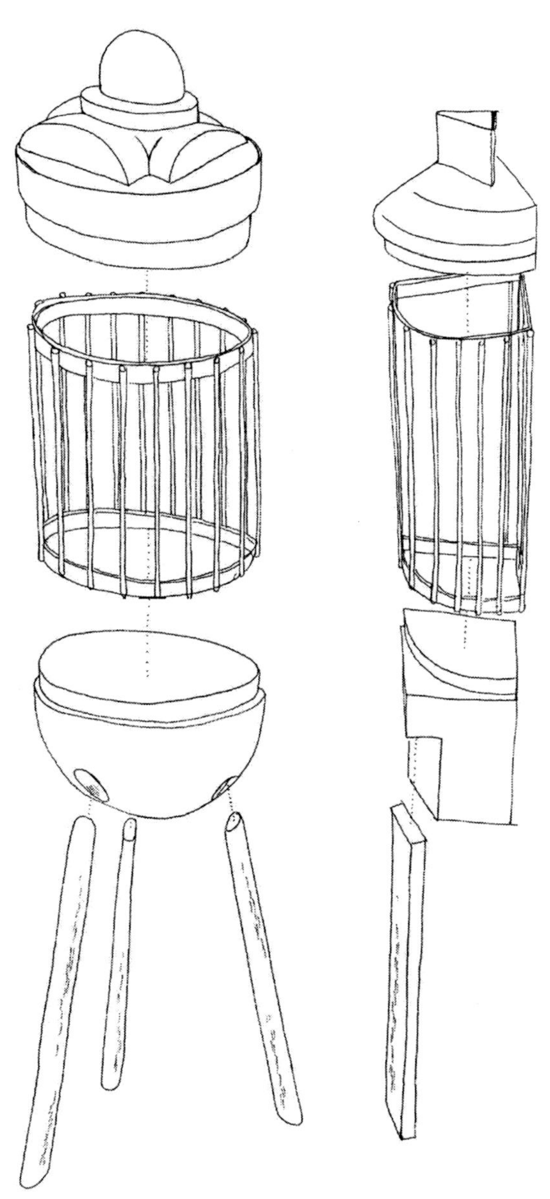

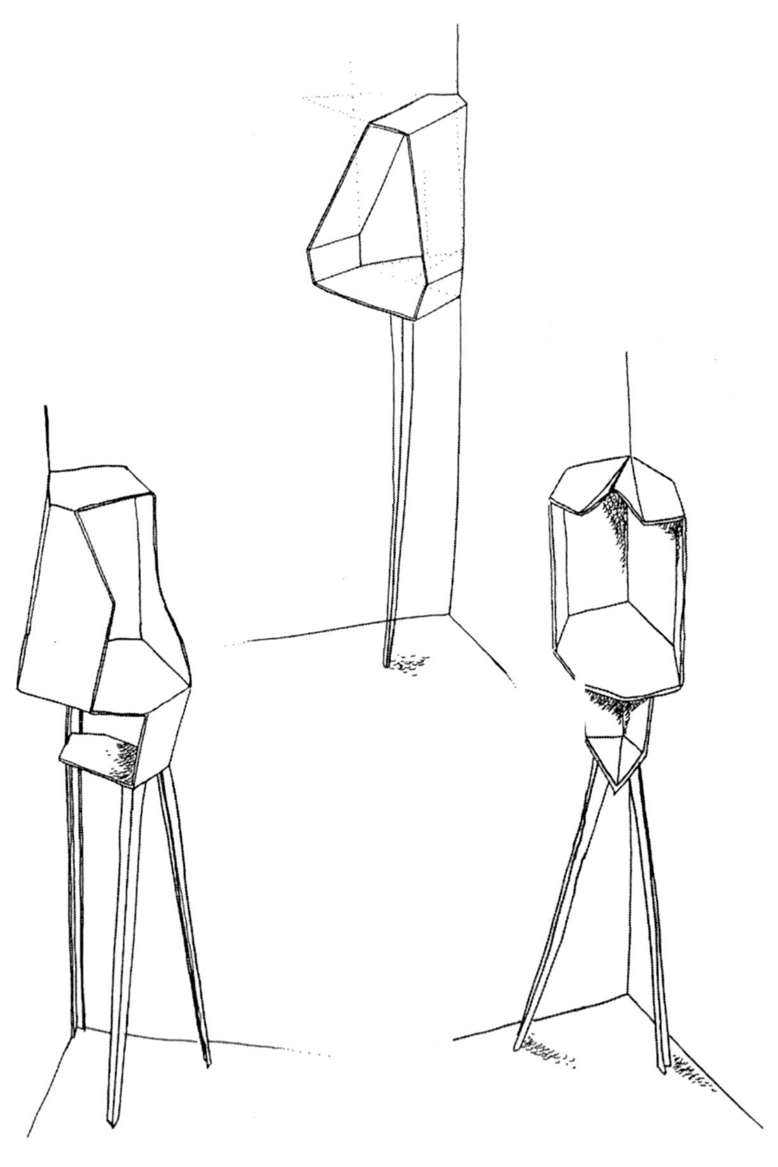

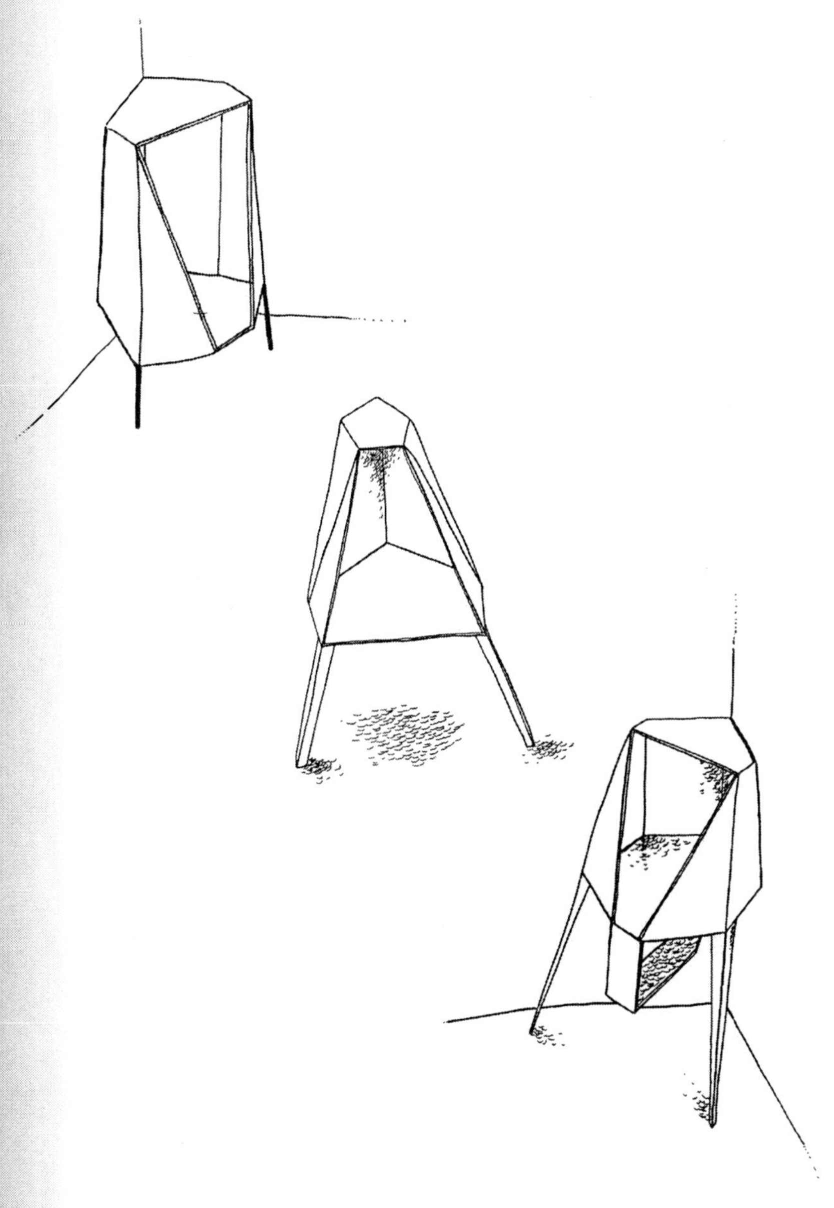

DRAWINGS TO COMPLETE

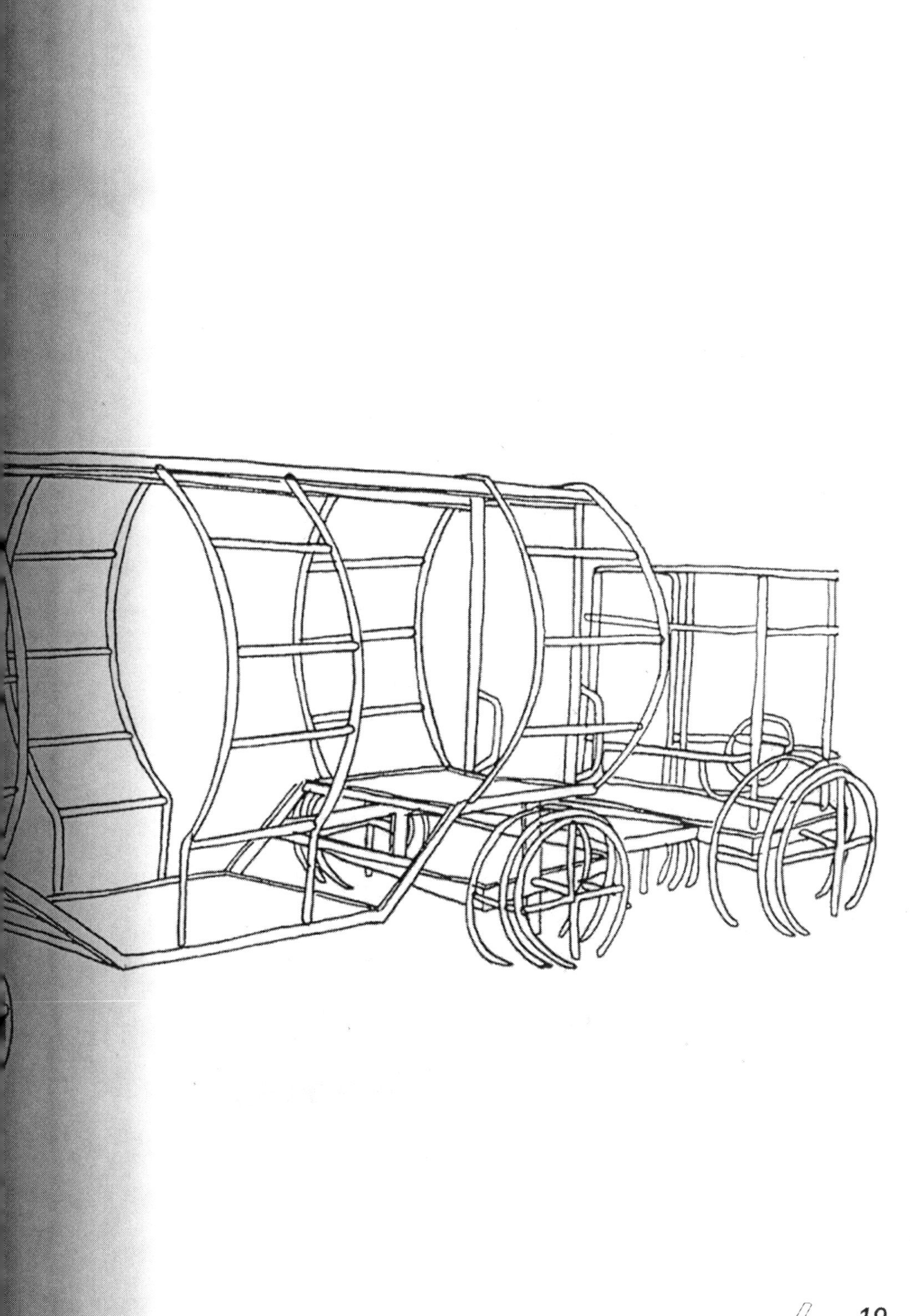

HOW IT IS

Most of the work has been made in thought, with hope, with quintals of drawings and a big fear of being wrong. From that, not so much has come. I am a tourist who keeps going on drawings and carefully I stay clear of making products. It is about the disability of considering other people's lives as an area to work from.

December 2007

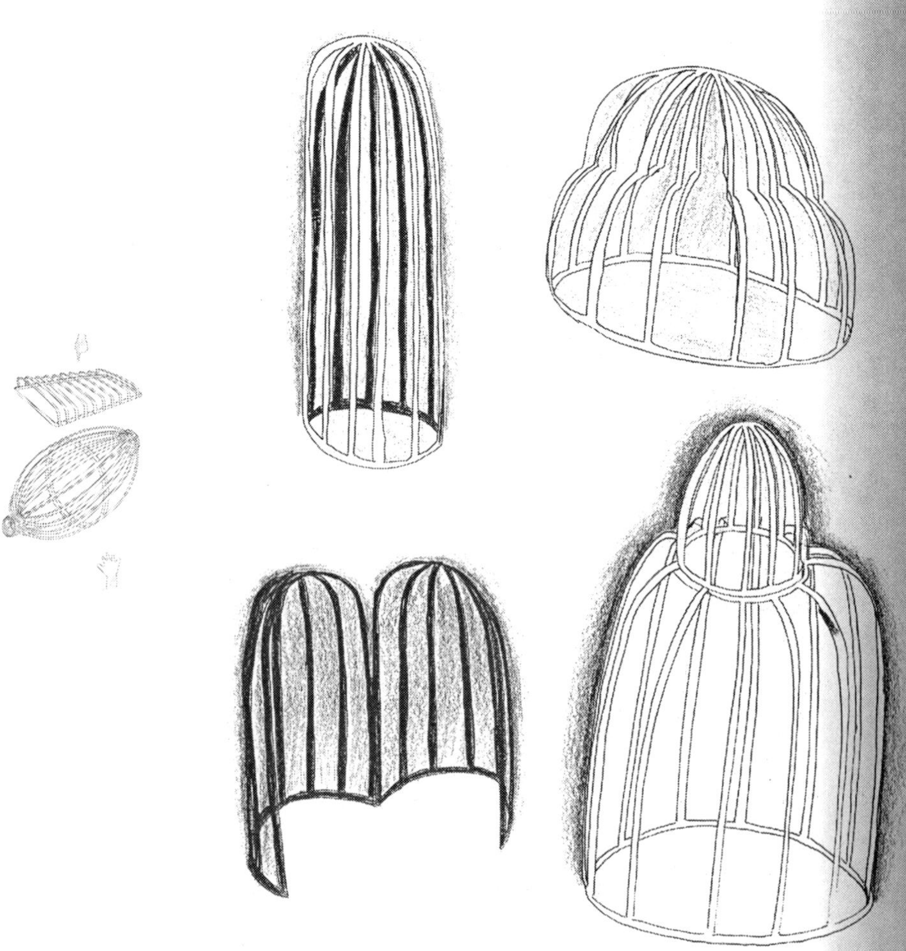

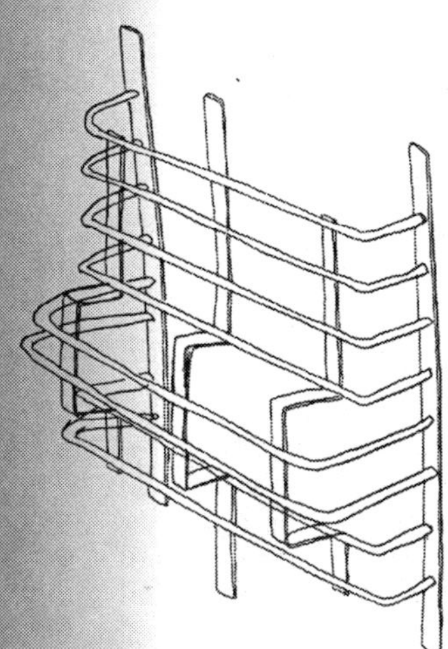

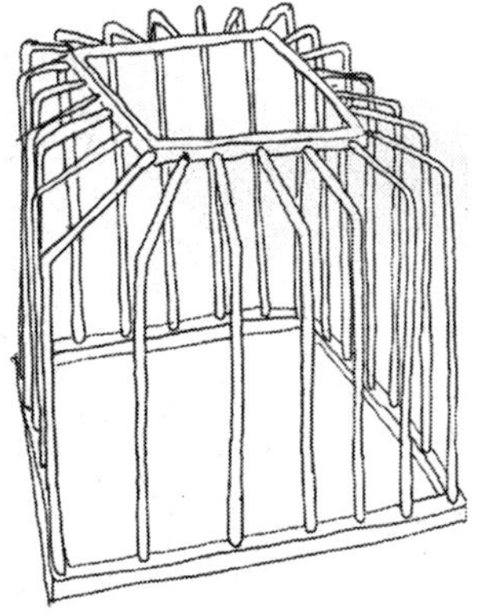

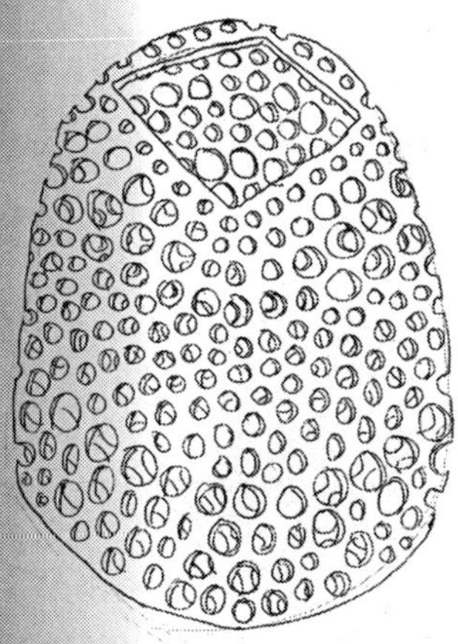

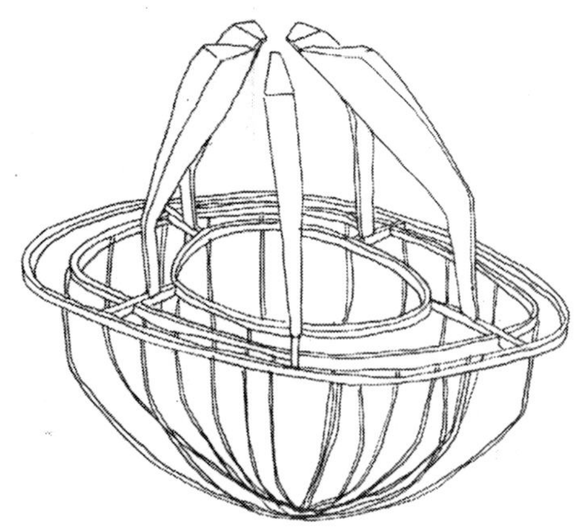

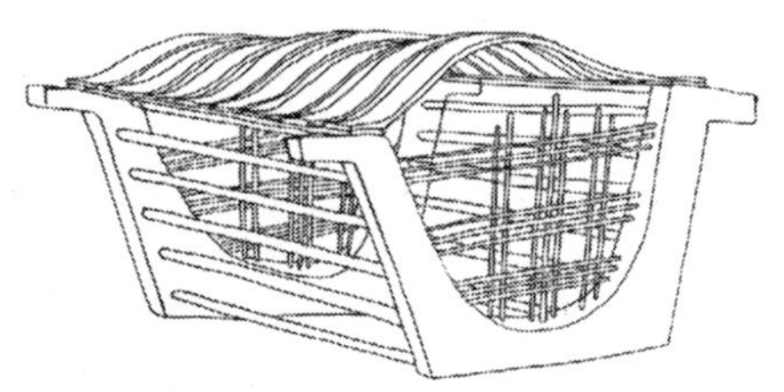

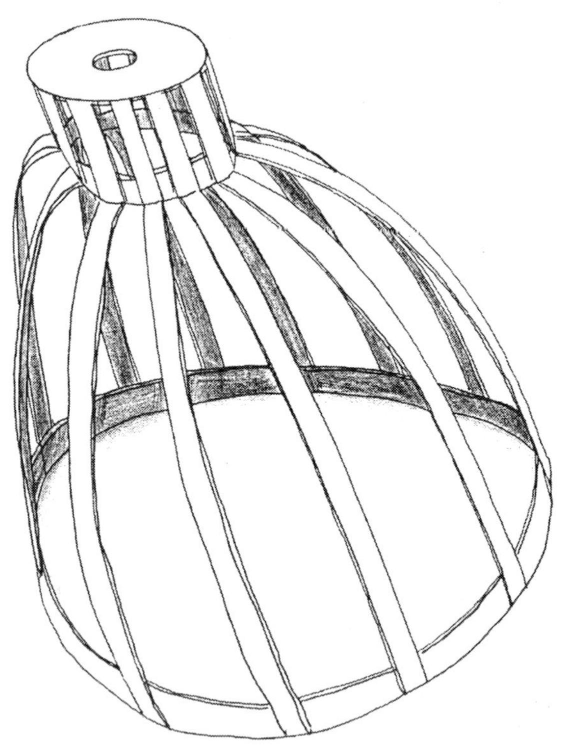

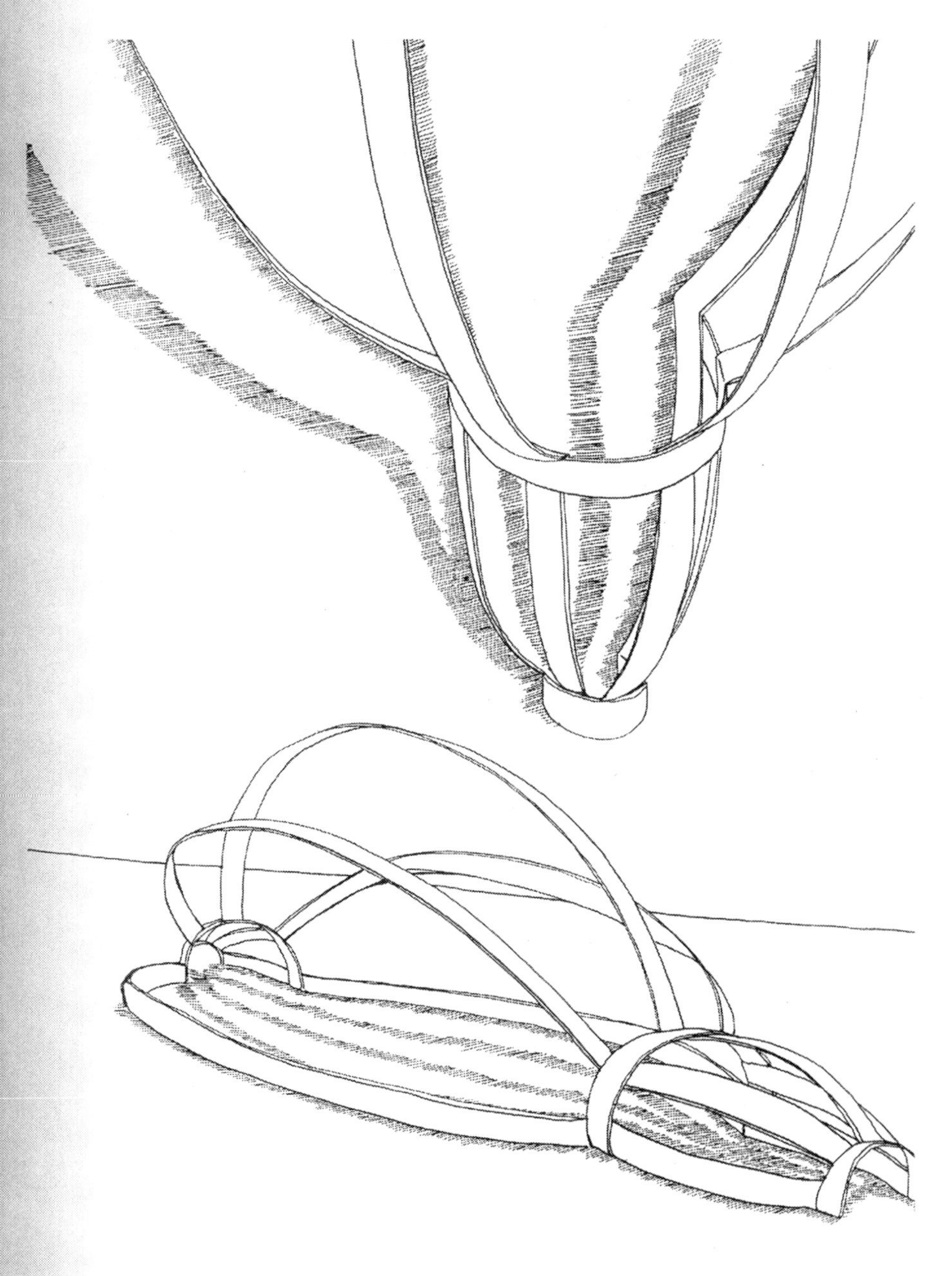

THE BEAR TRAP

The 'Stone Bear Trap' is the best machine to kill. The most dangerous and the most terrifying because it never fails its morbid goal even with its appearance of a sweet celtic sculpture.

The bear arrives by himself, he is even searching for it because he can smell from afar the scent of the honey puddle placed under a heavy stone held by the tree. The honey flavour turns the bear crazy. He looses his mind from the moment he licks it. He help himself because there is no more honey to look for. But before he finishes he will be dead. The reason is because of the stone which hits his head each time the bear stands up after each lick. He will kill himself by cranial injury. Mistrust the seductive objects that you absolutely want to approach.

April 2008

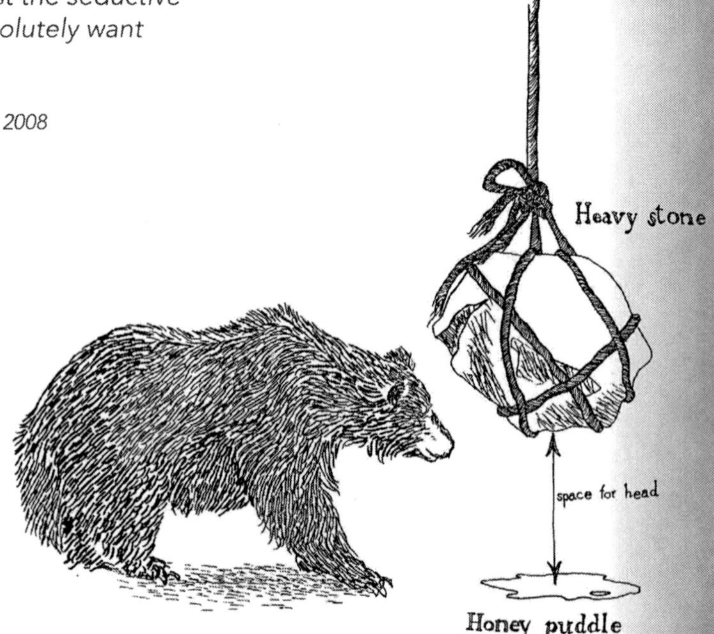

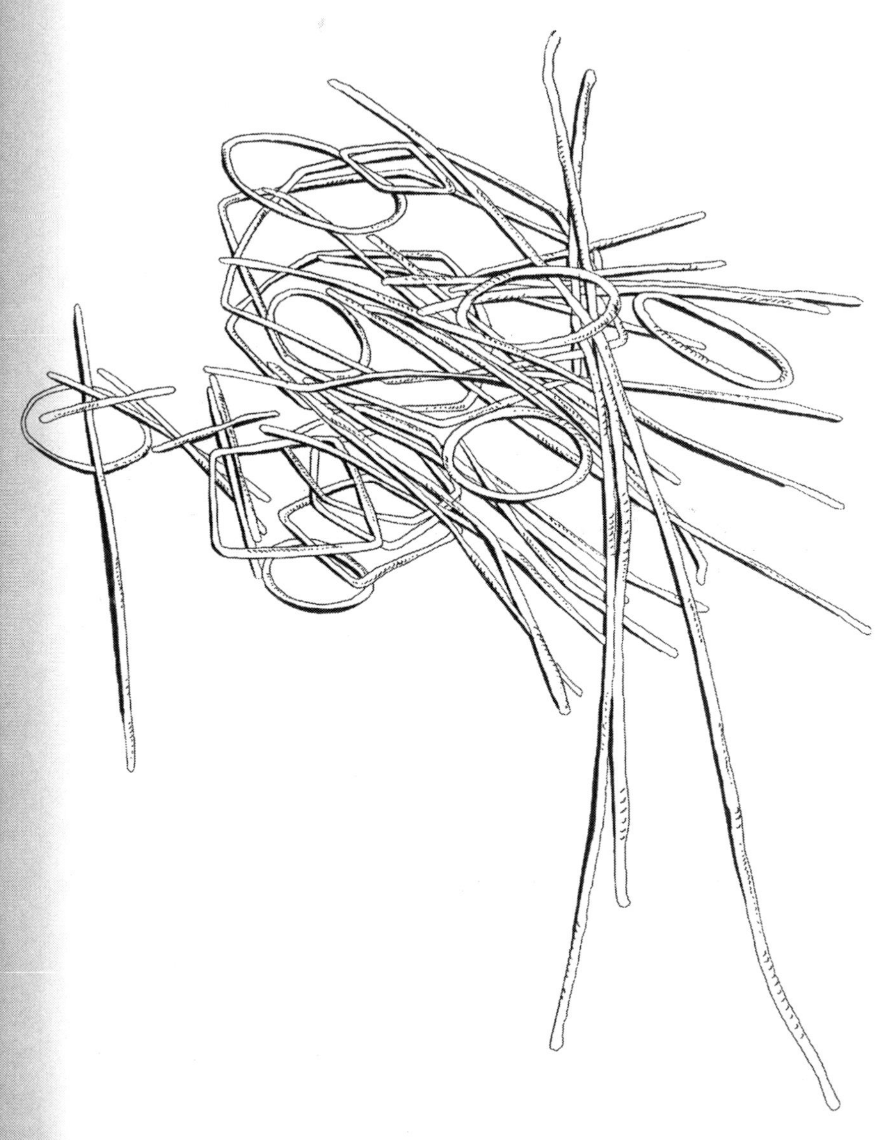

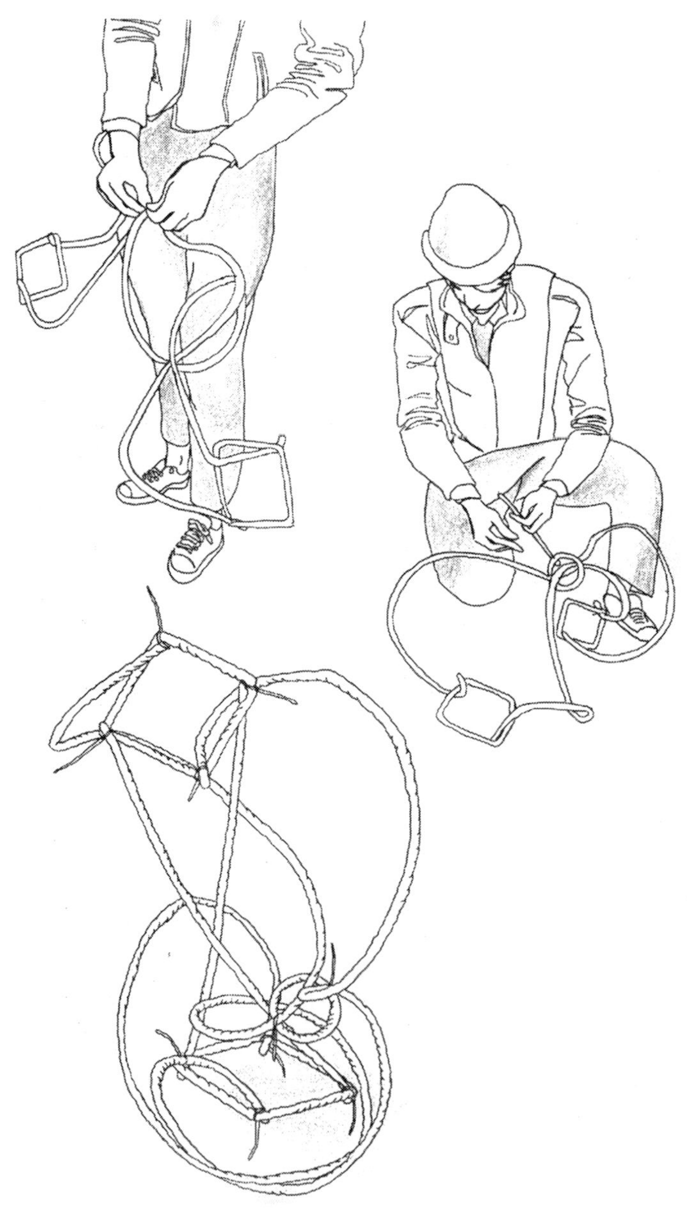

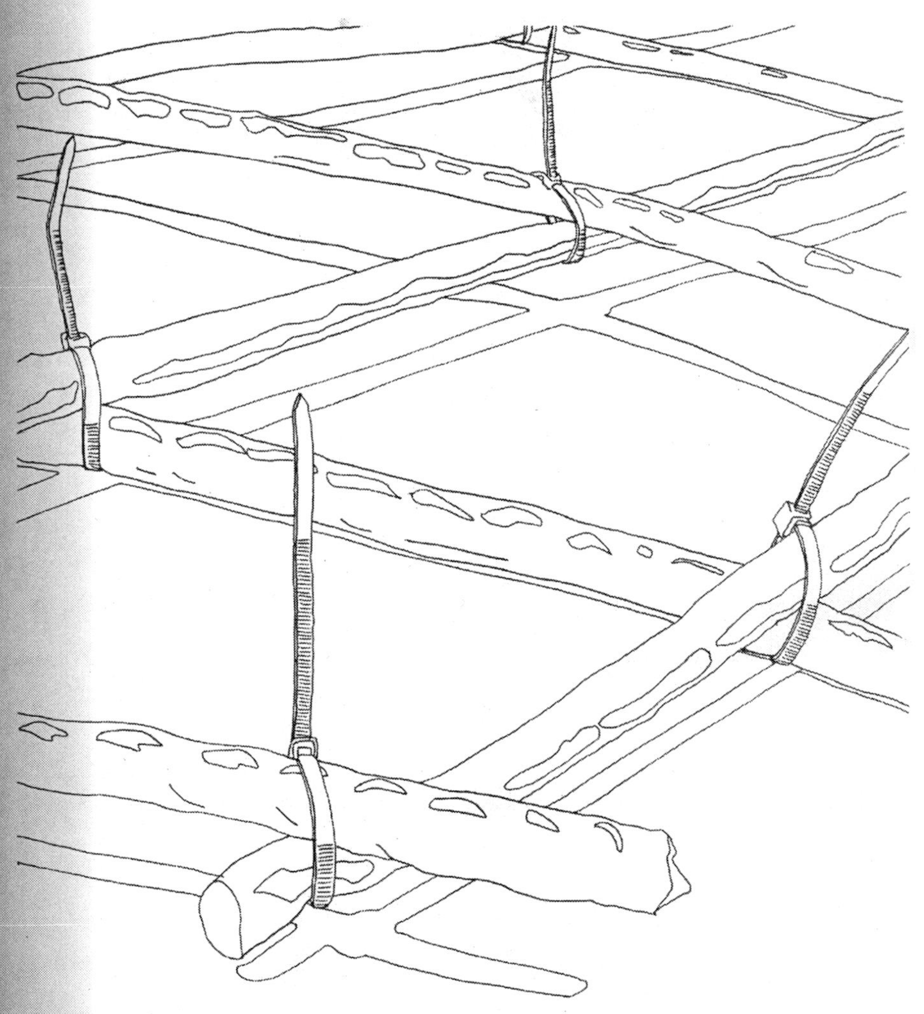

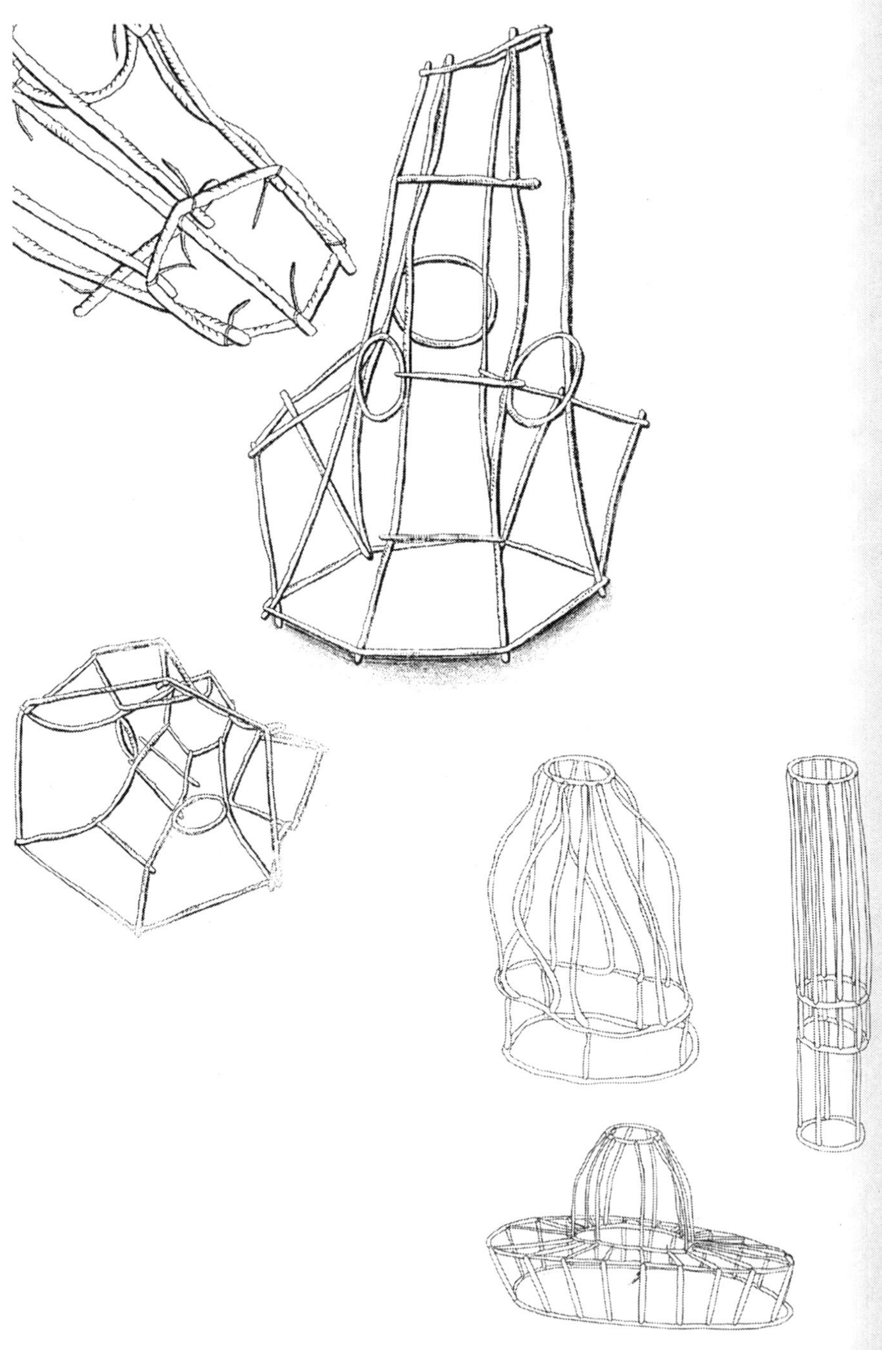

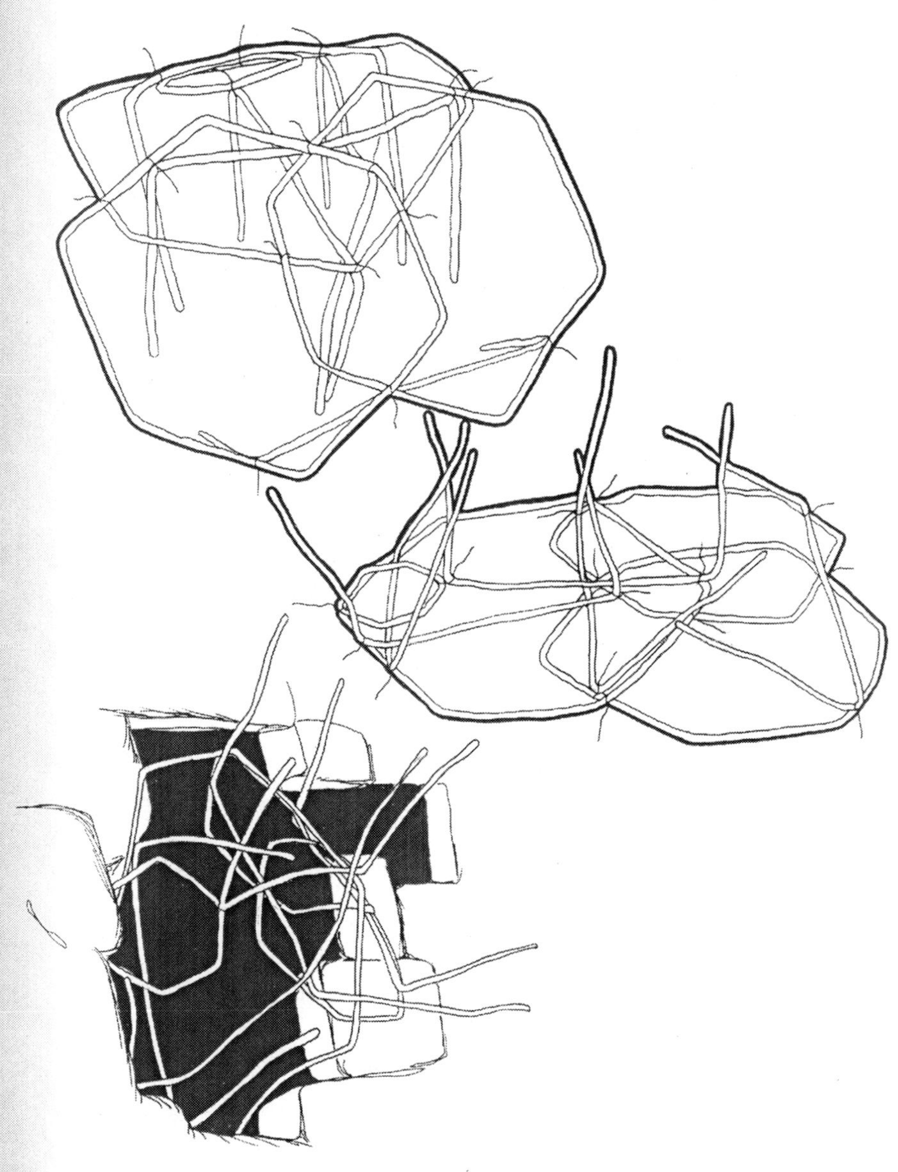

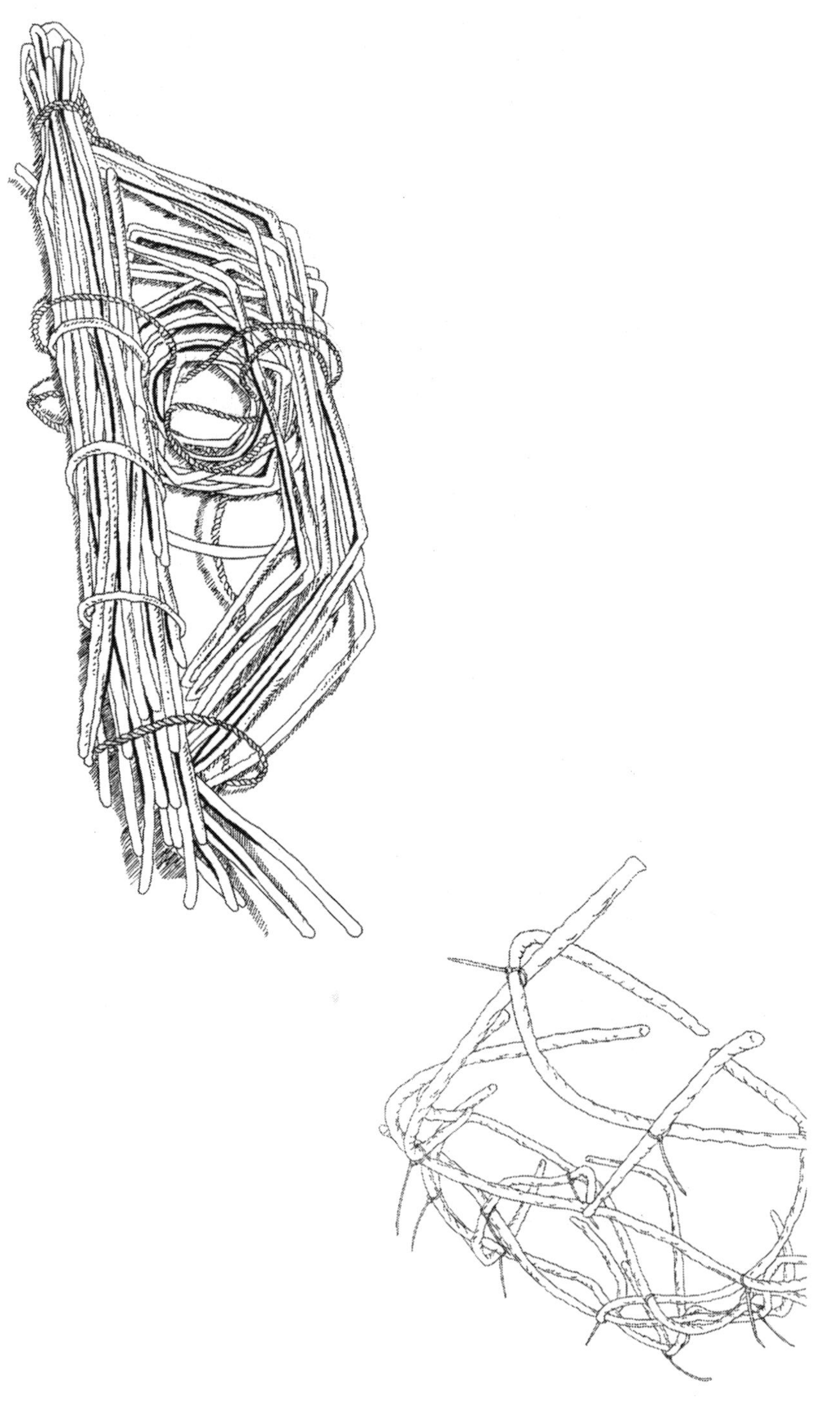

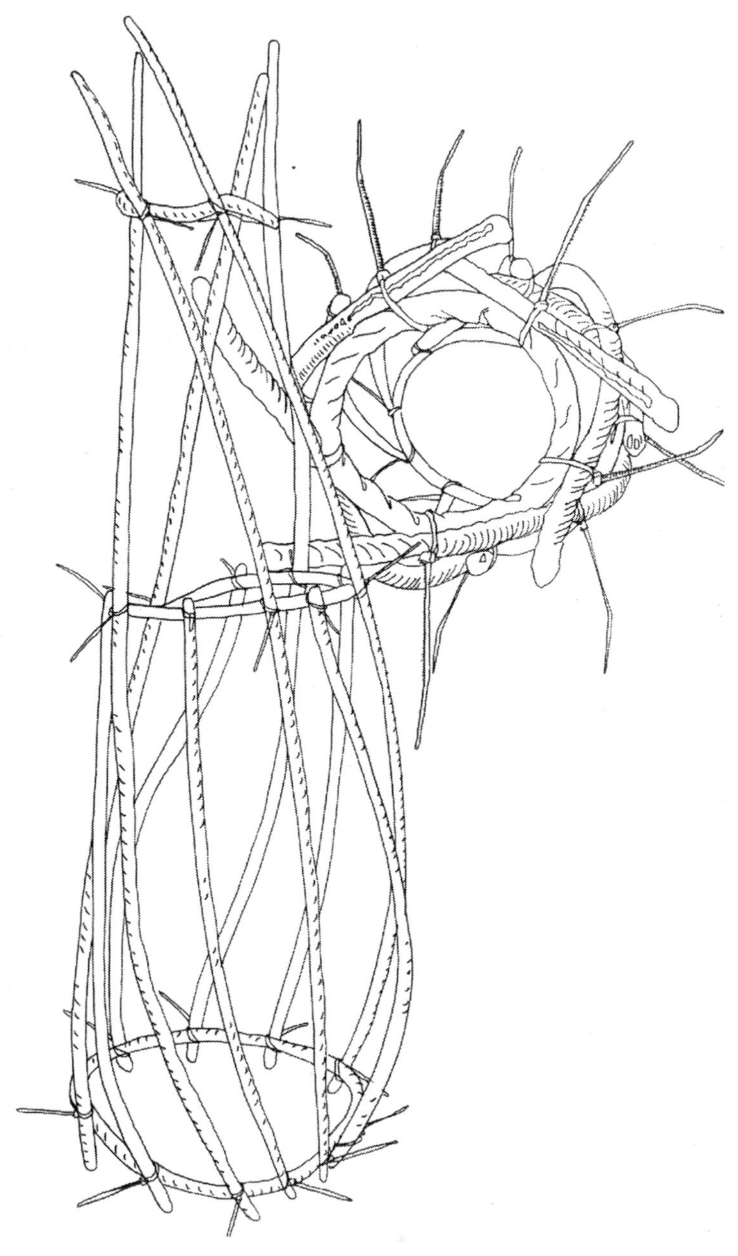

THE COLLEGE THAT WE DESIRE

I am going to college because I know that there I will shape my mind. I do my work on my own and get some opinions from my two 'sages'. They are used to saying a lot. They talk about other things but then, bit by bit, they tell stories which, if I am alert enough, should make me realise what is wrong with my work. They offer me thoughts. They encourage me to think about all the things that come before and behind a notion. They educate me to think that a thousand engineering manuals do not bring to realisation any single design.

The college that we desire first assumes its insufficiency in producing a truly global education, the one that pushes us out onto the highway of the unknown ground, where doubt forms and finds an application. In the most radical way, the college should kick the student out. But that cannot come from we students, because it is hard to leave the flattery system. I do my best to stay in the 'room' because I know that it will finish soon. It is hard to perceive from an individual view the personal benefit of collective investigation. It is hard to see why I should put myself in difficulty to enrich the project; it is hard to see our project becoming a data-base for the rest of the group, and a lot of other 'it is hard to' scenarios…

January 2008

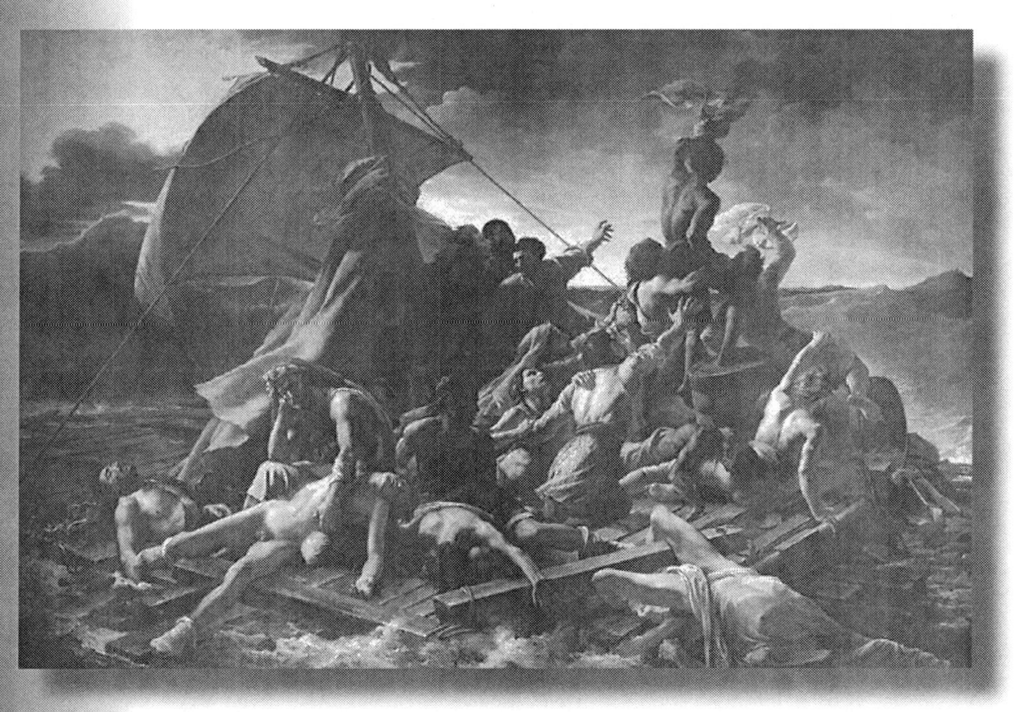

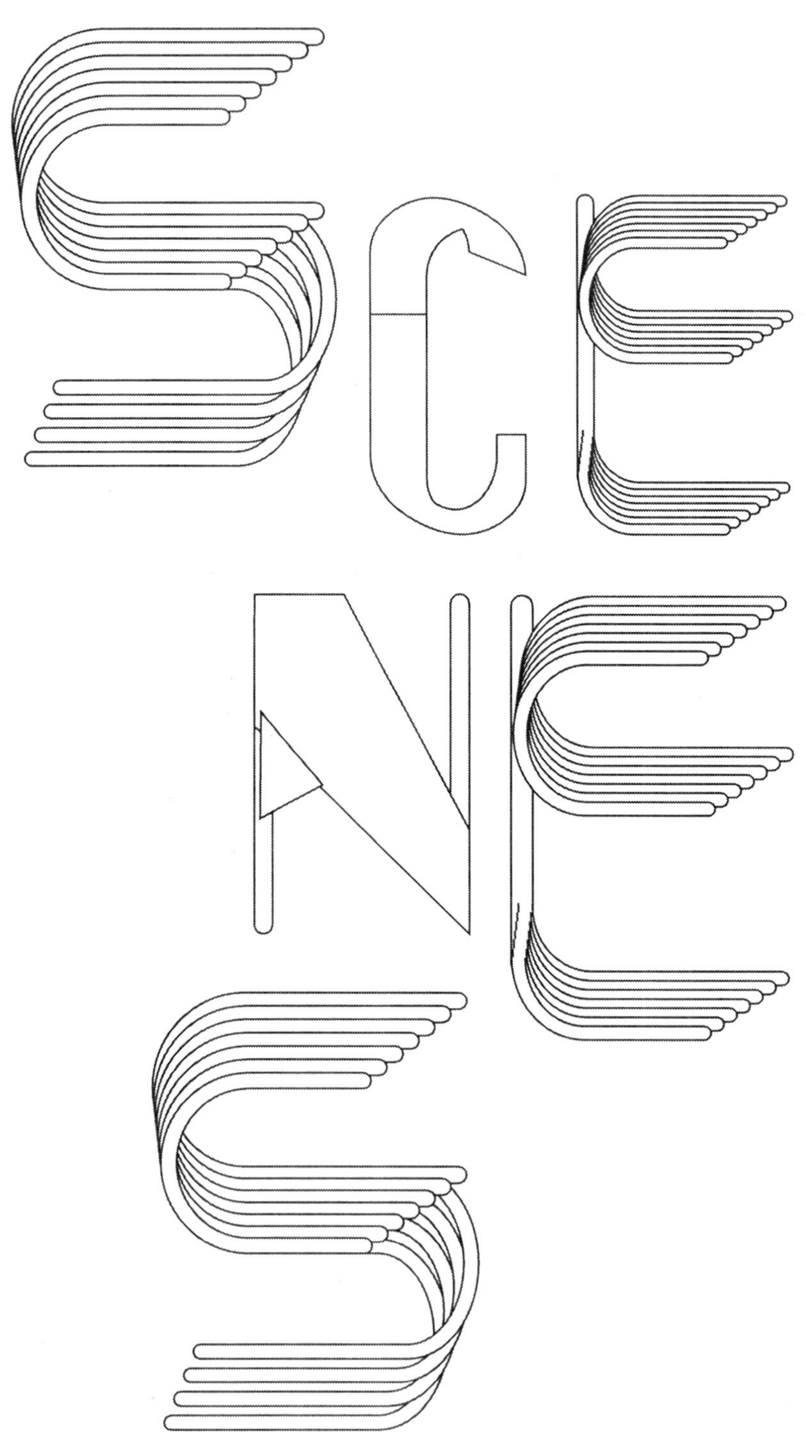

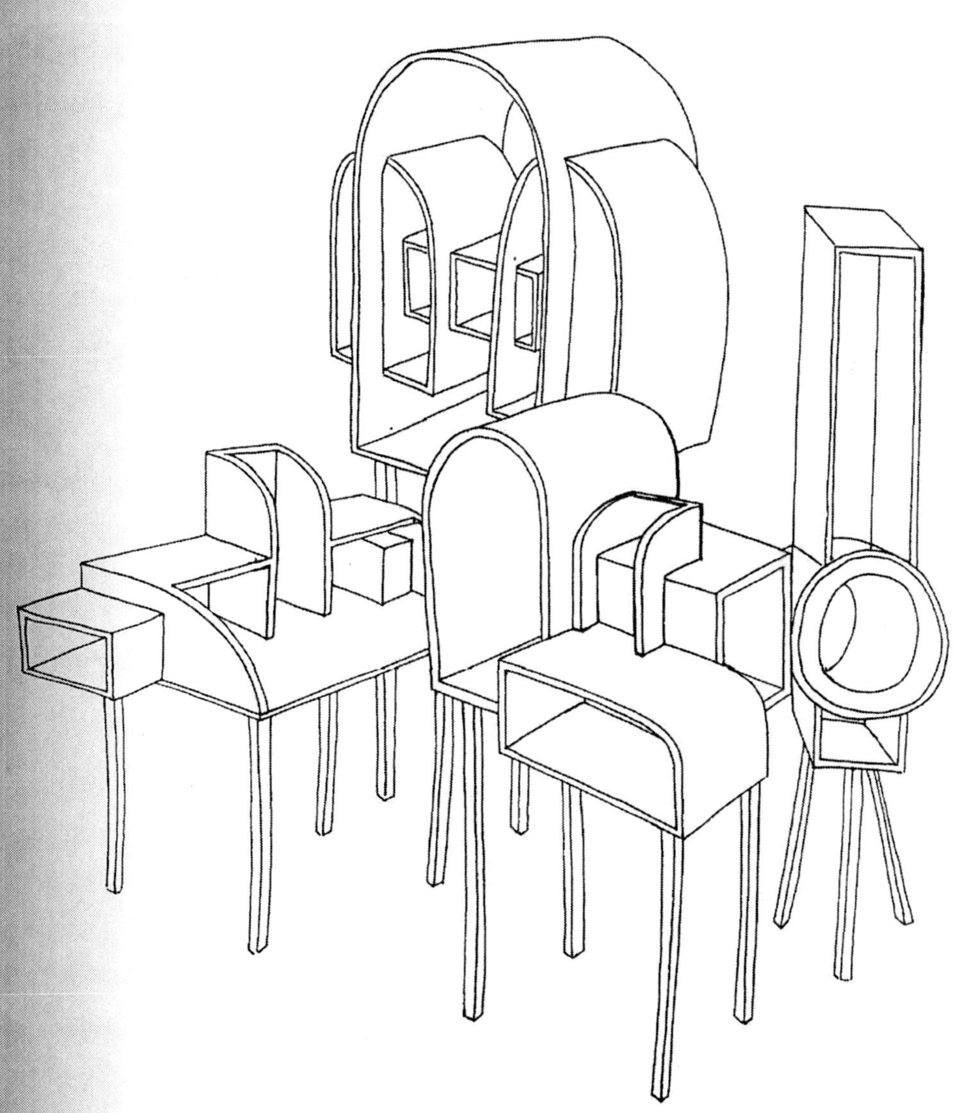

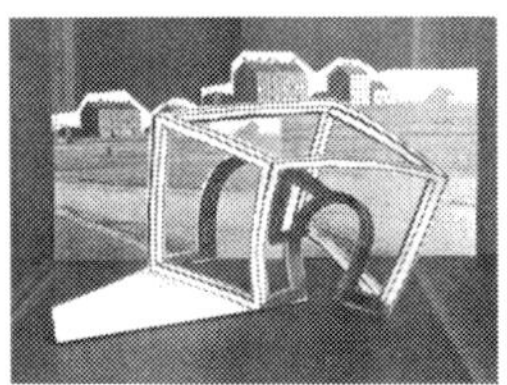

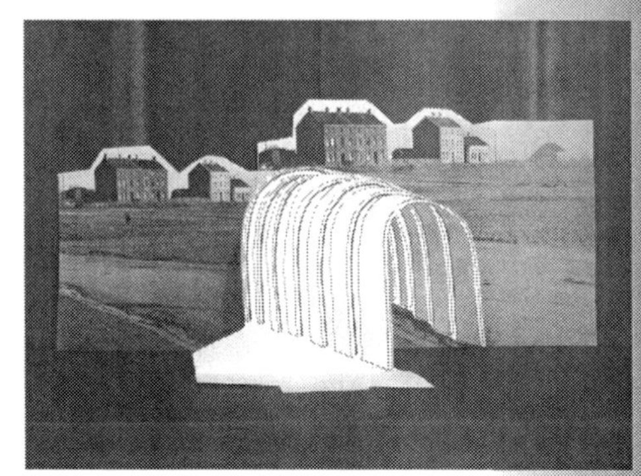

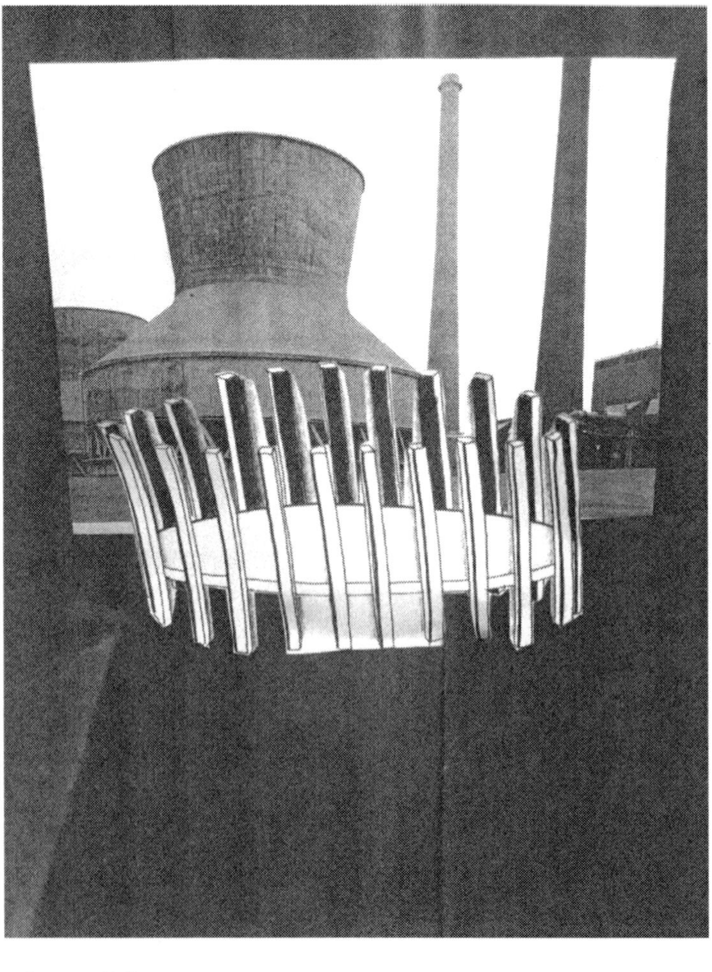

HOW IT SHOULD BE

It should be about the possibility of people's creativity other than my own, to feel that these forms make me happy and that they can make other people happy.

It should be about the integration of these forms into a specific context, a context which is around where I am: the street, the park, the flat of Mister X, the crossing light, the bench on the corner, the space between the bathroom and the stairs. These are the geographical context, just as there are the happening contexts: two woman targeting the same seat on the bus, passing through the park instead of taking the underground, being late for an appointment, hesitating between an ice-cream and a tiramisu, or taking both, having dinner in the bed, not going to sleep tonight ... A situation, a way of living, as a site for the creation of objects.

It should be a dialogue between forms extracted from a private drawing-book and the 'community', the other, the group. These forms would inform my idea of place, my idea of object, my idea of an object in a place, and my idea of we ourselves amongst these objects, in place. It should be a place, an object, and people.

It should be a lot of production without breaks. As the drawings come more easily, the making and the exploration of places and contexts should be more generous. It should be a large document of these forms in many situations. That should be my process, the one I feel comfortable with, because I use the tools that I control.

It should come as a reflection of the possibility of an object: the idea of somebody taking possession of this object, the idea that the object should suggest comfort (material and/or mental) for the owner. It should come as more specific research about one form, in one place. When the possibility of an object exists, it should also involve other people to bring it into reality. This should be the slow process, the one which consists of dialogue with a person or group of people possessing a knowledge that I don't have.

December 2007

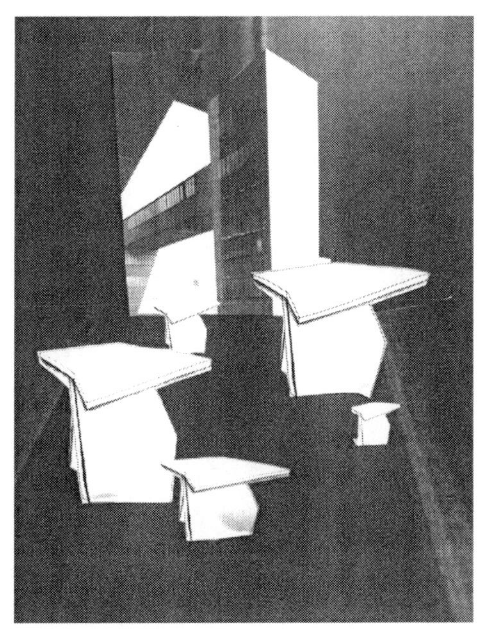

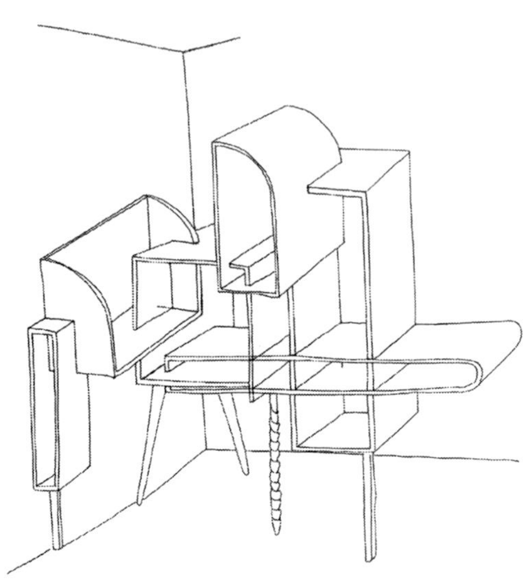

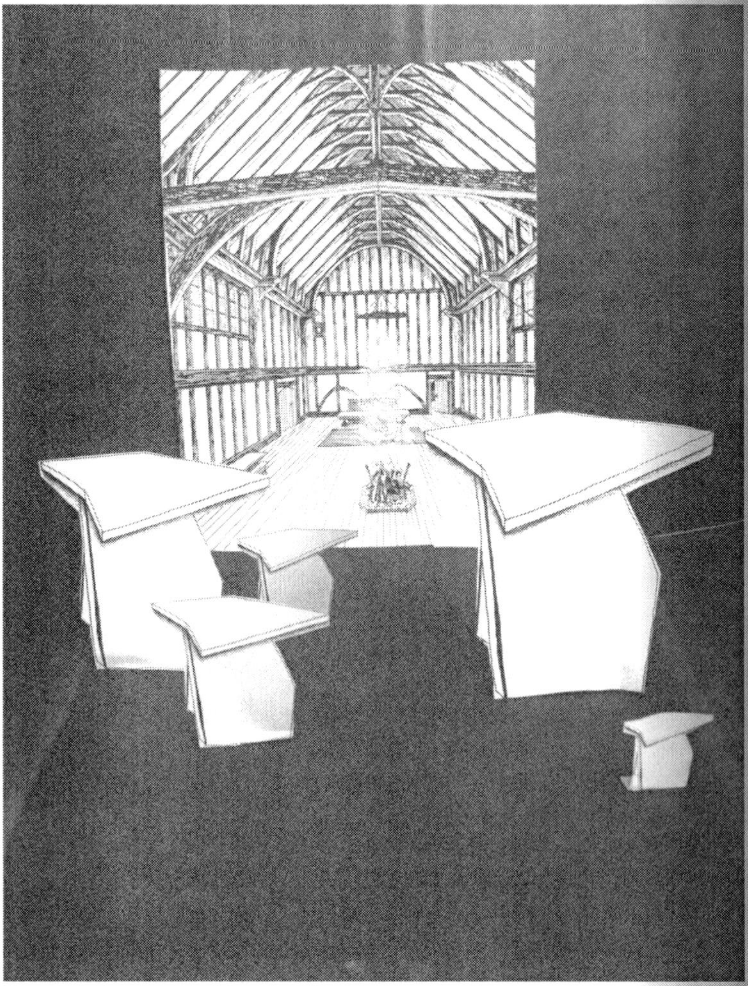

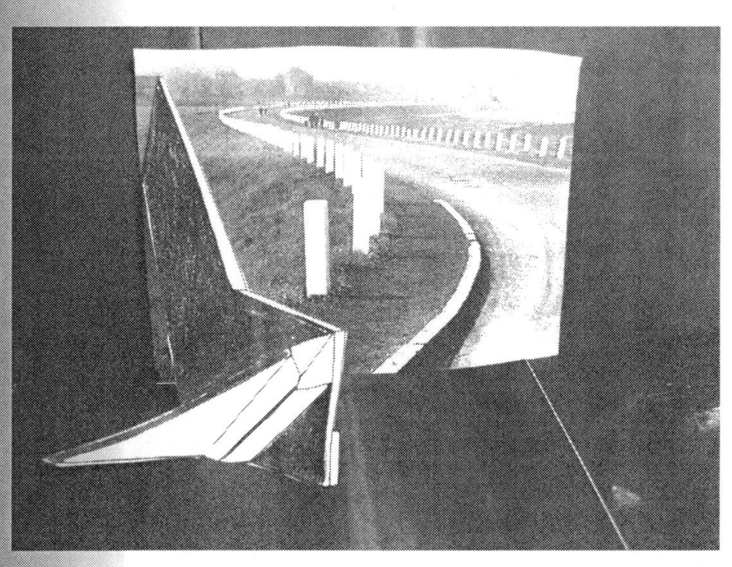

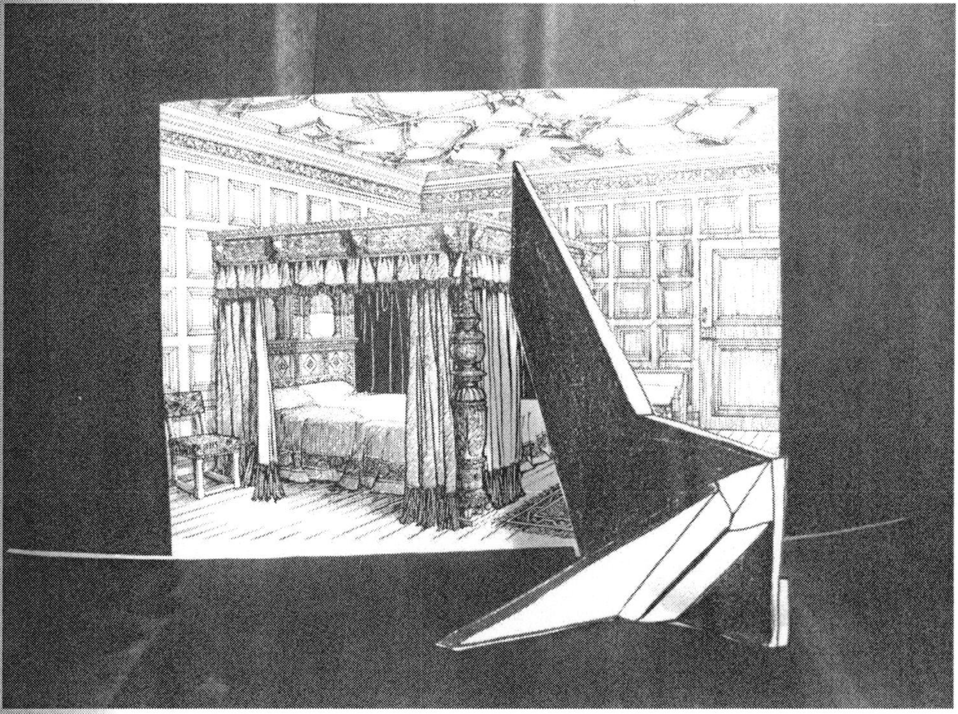

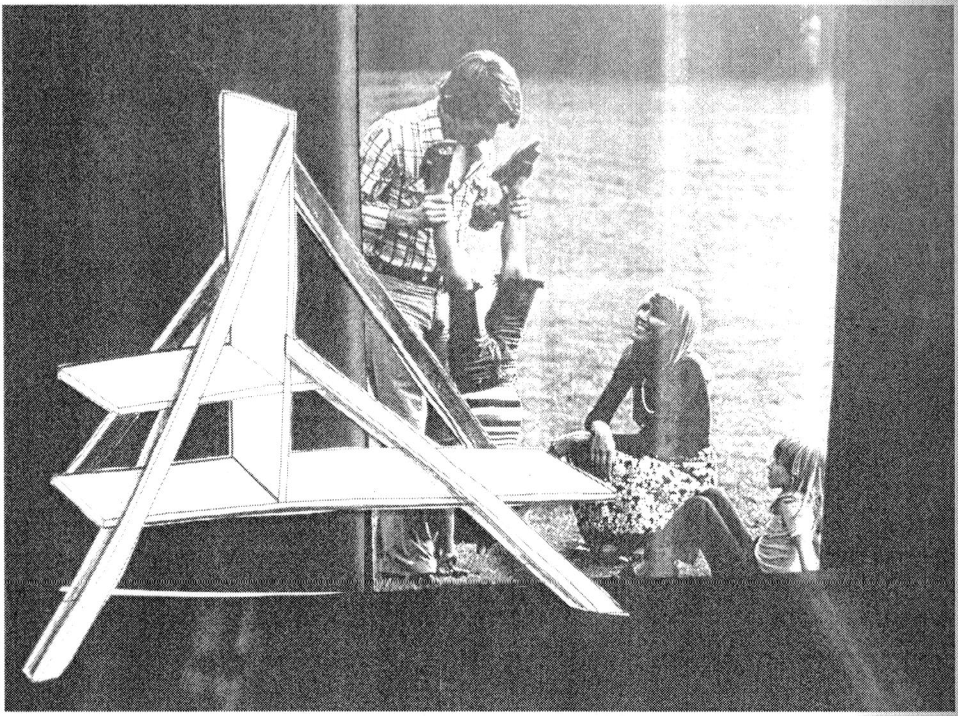

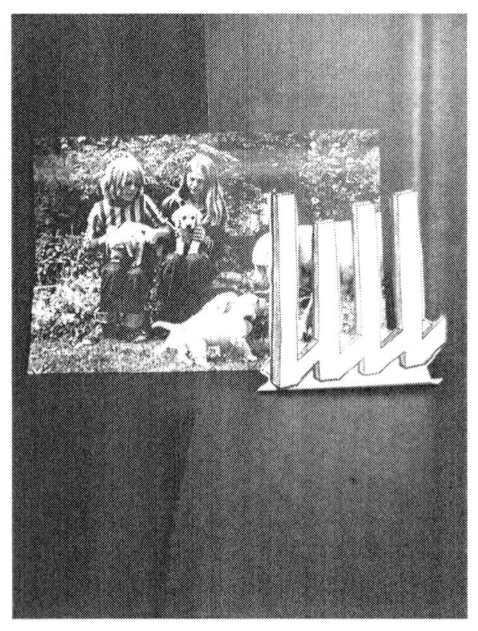

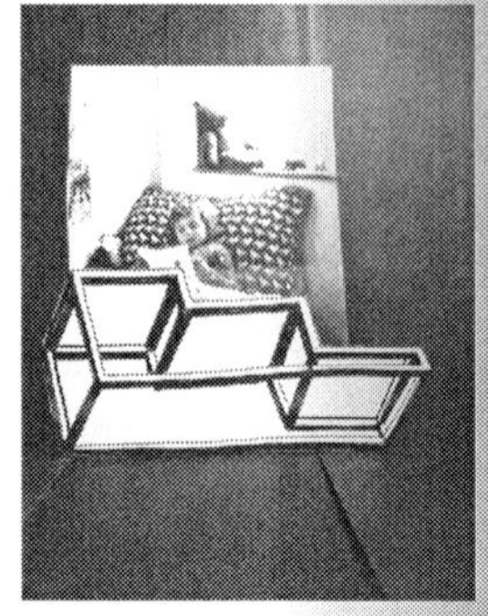

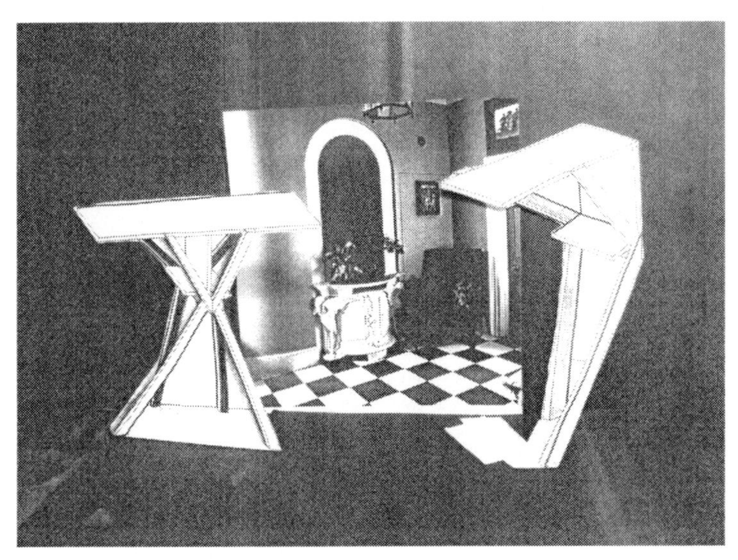

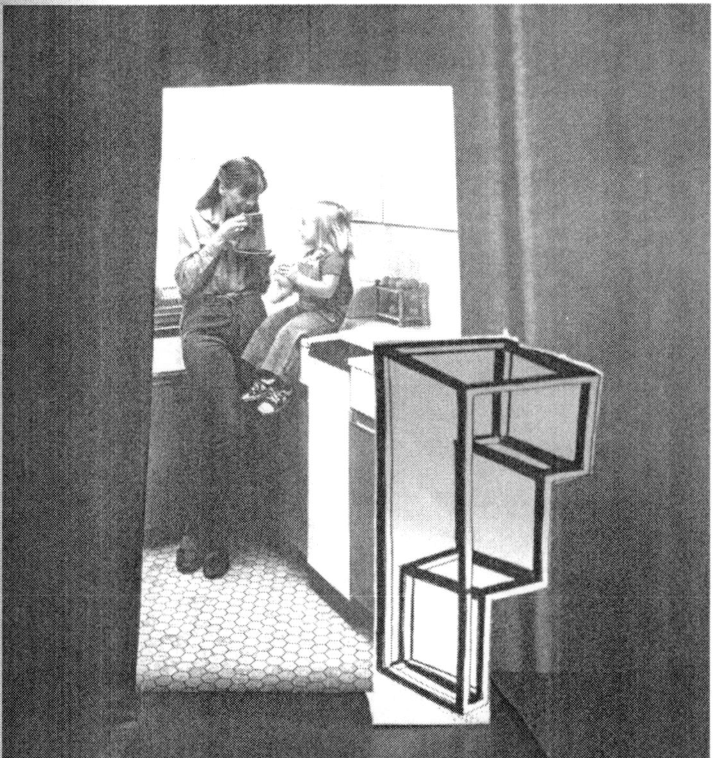

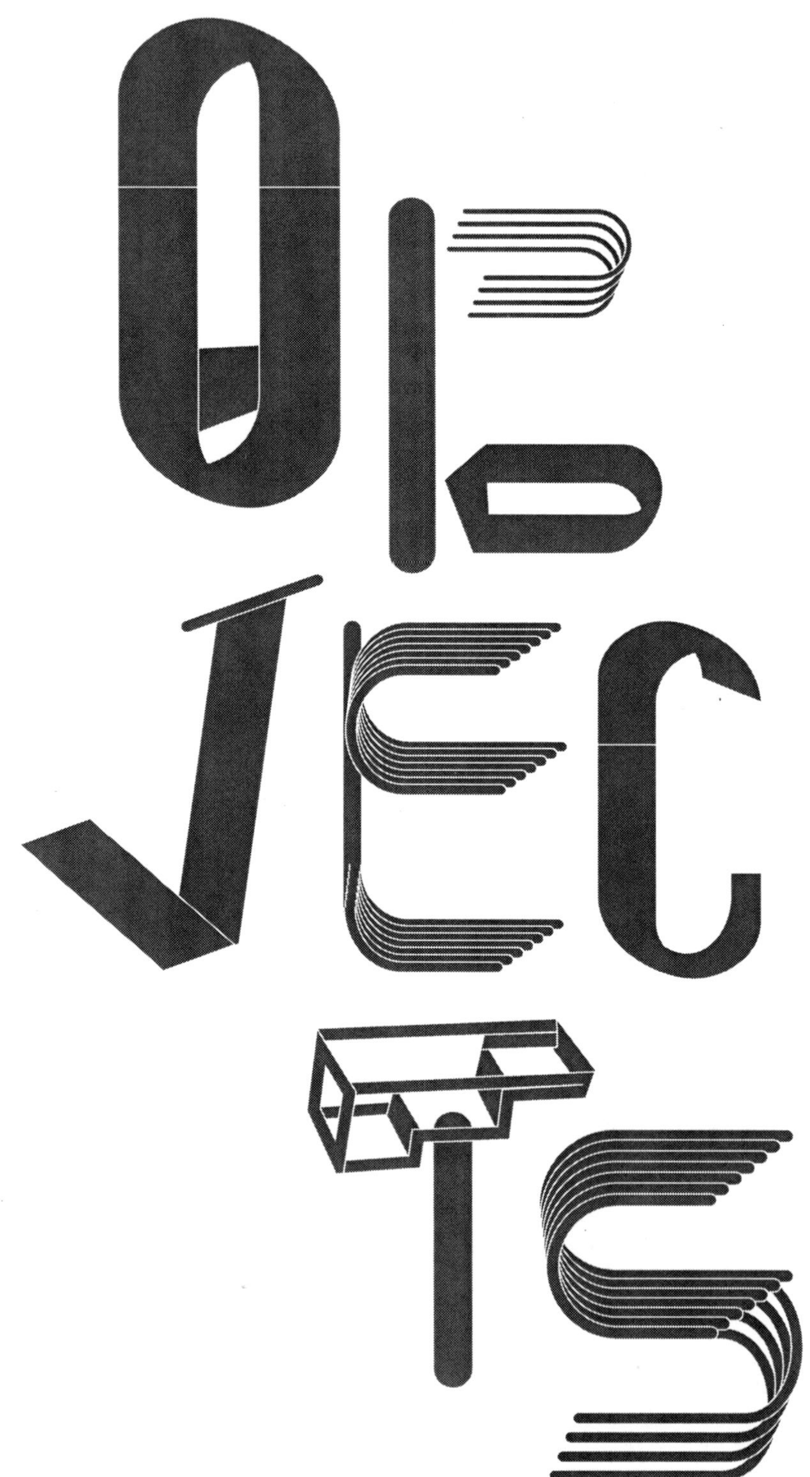

OBJECTS

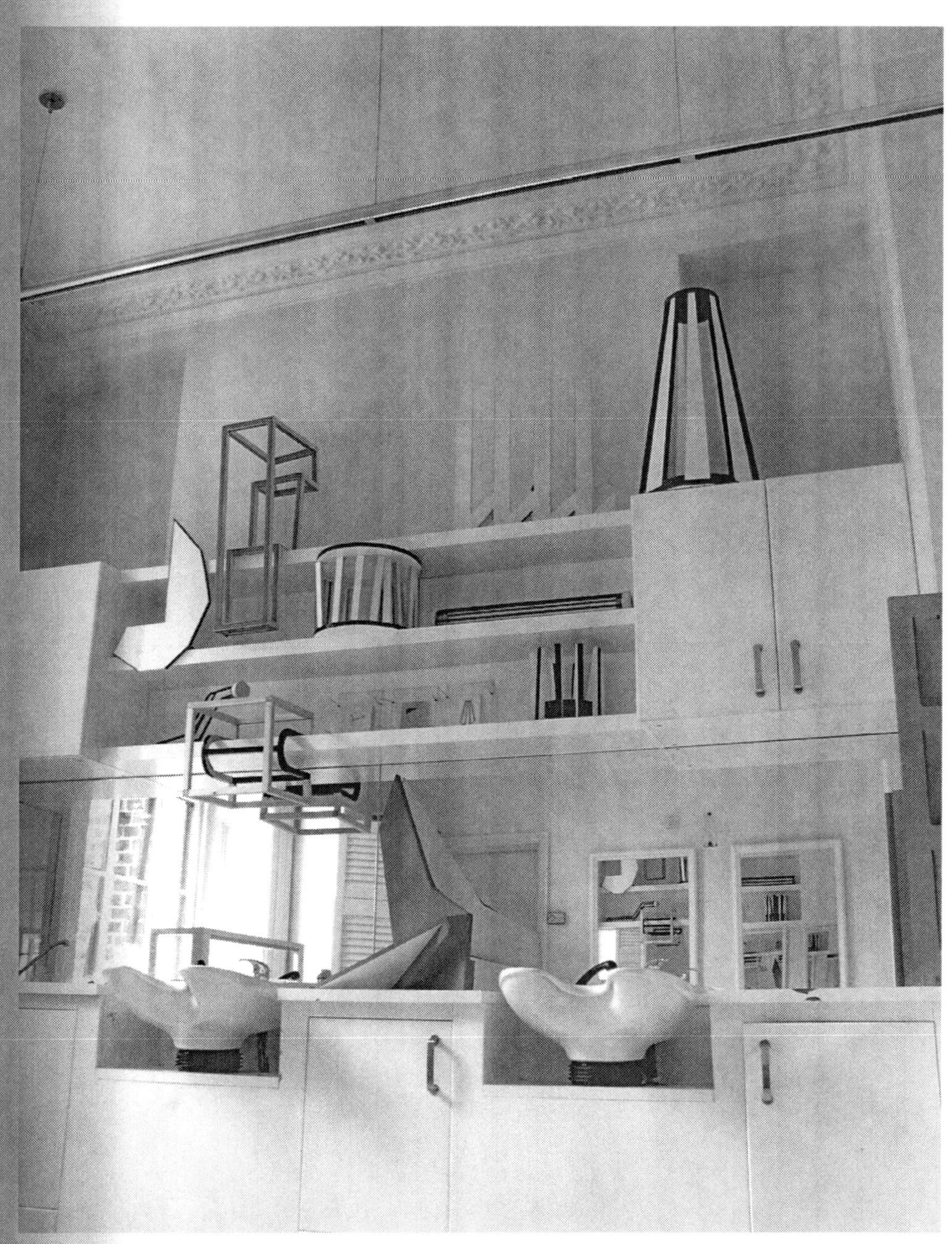

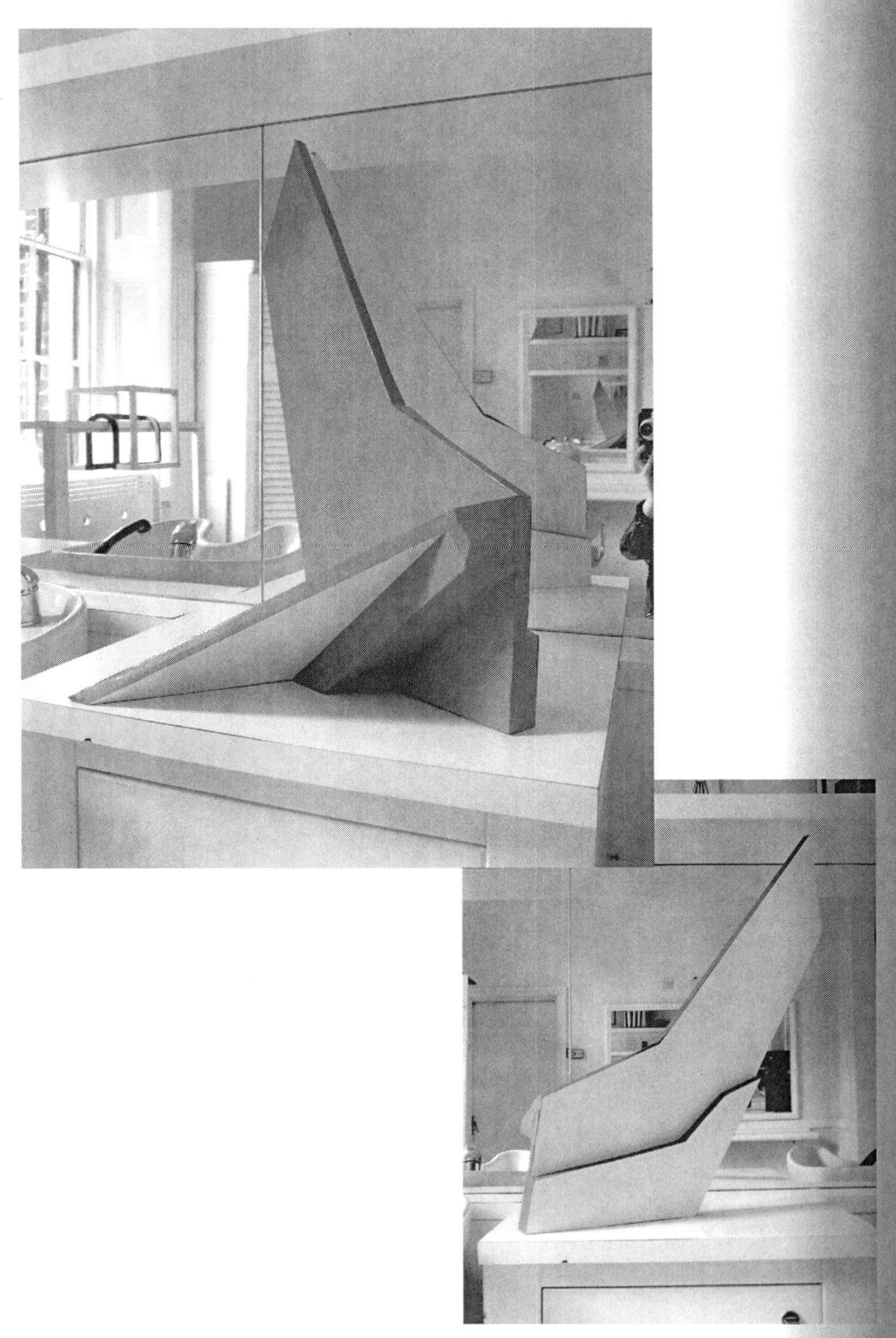

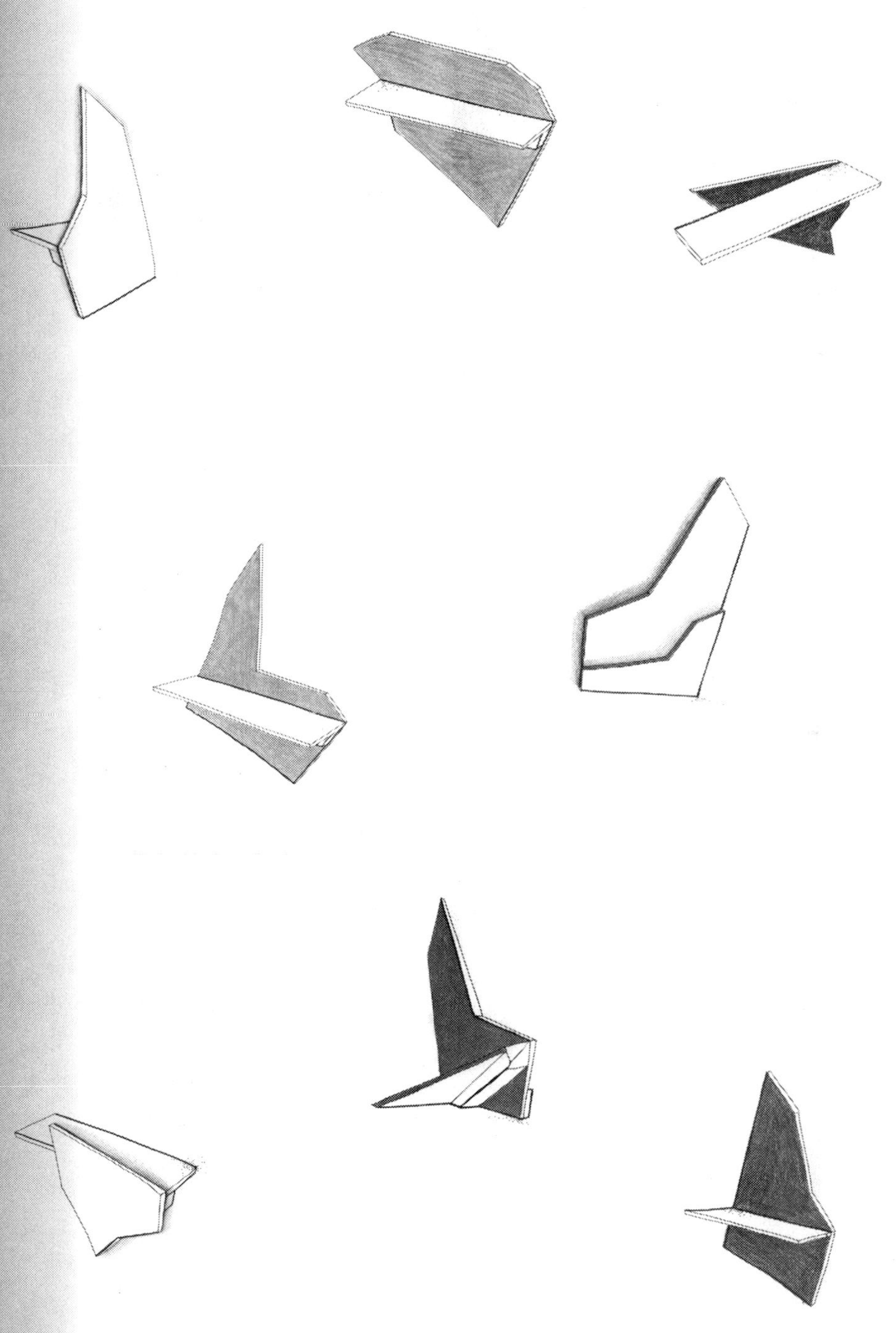

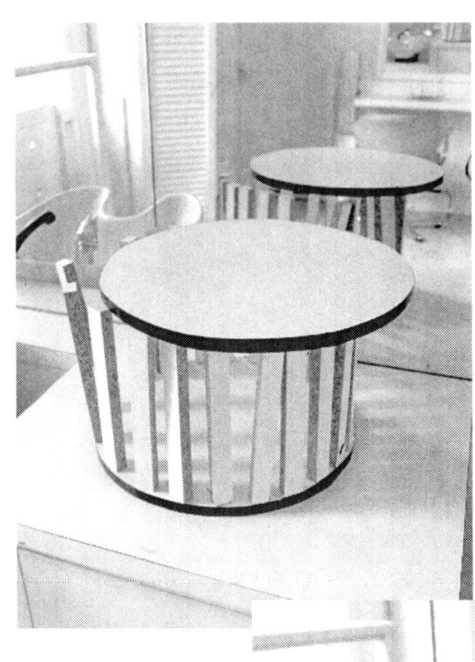

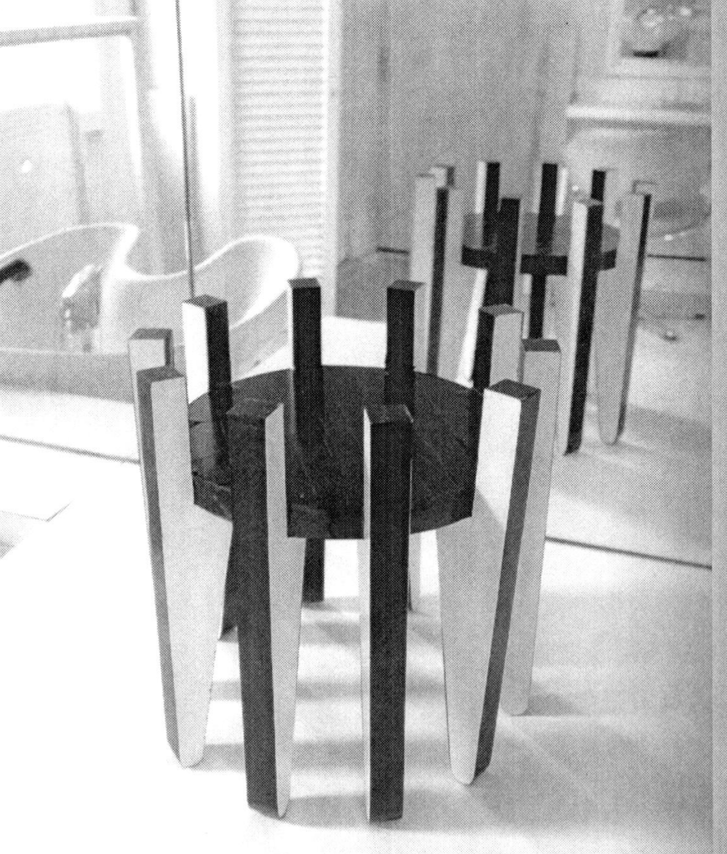

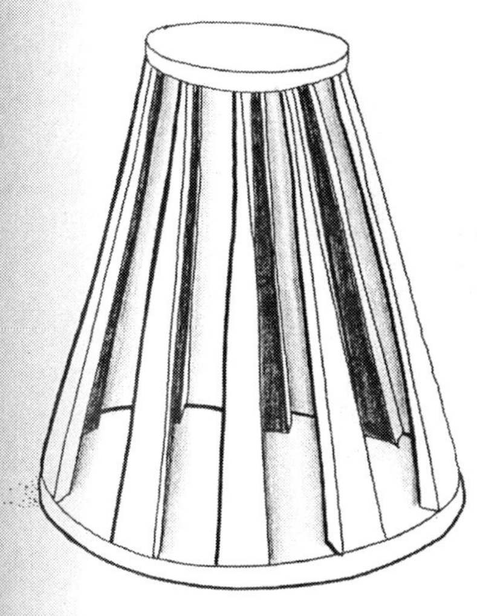

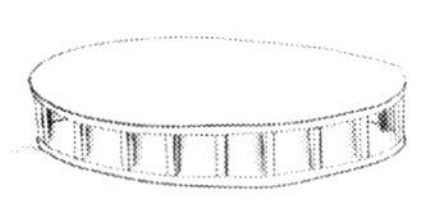

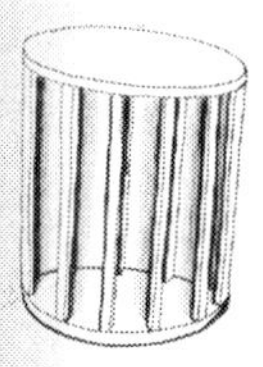

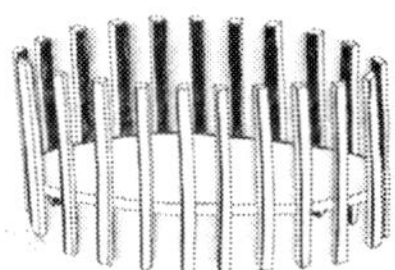

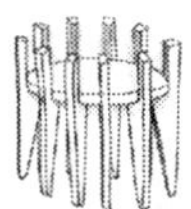

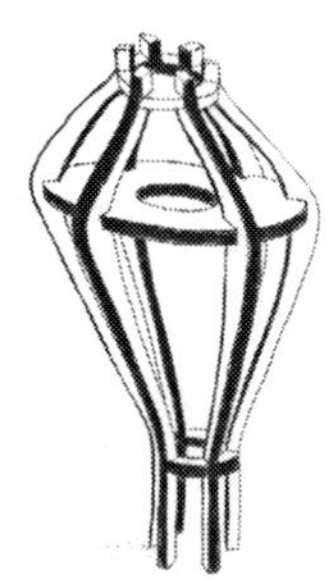

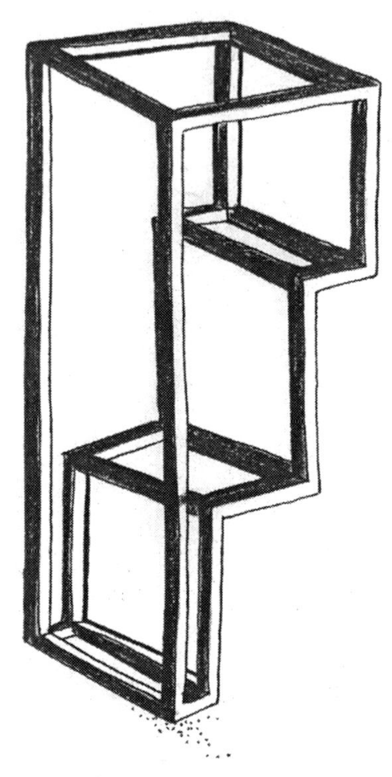

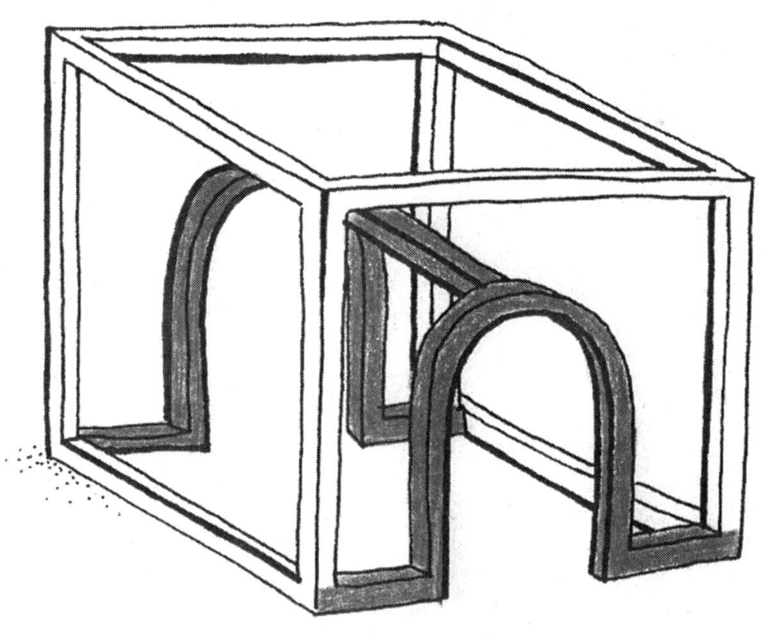

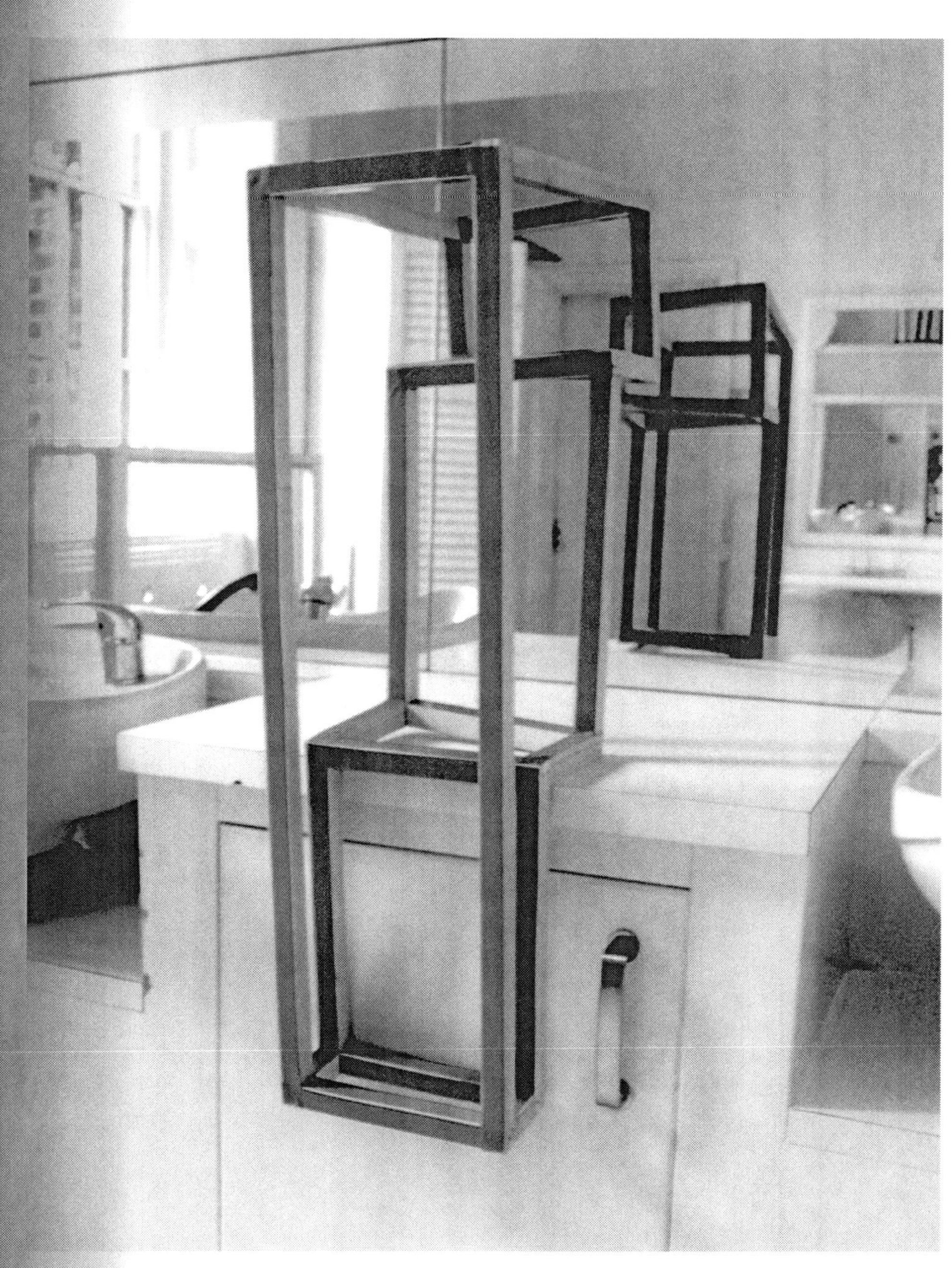

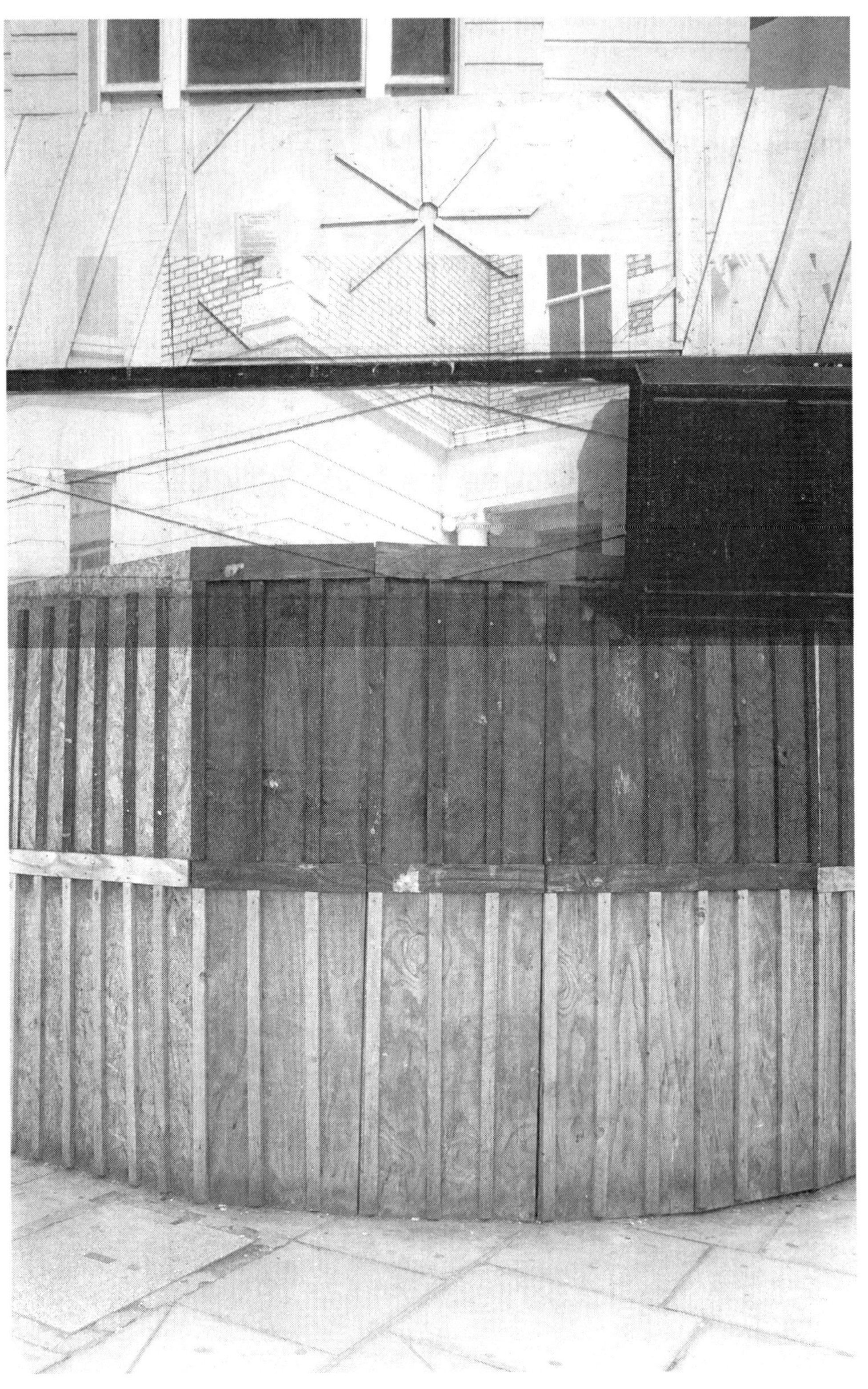

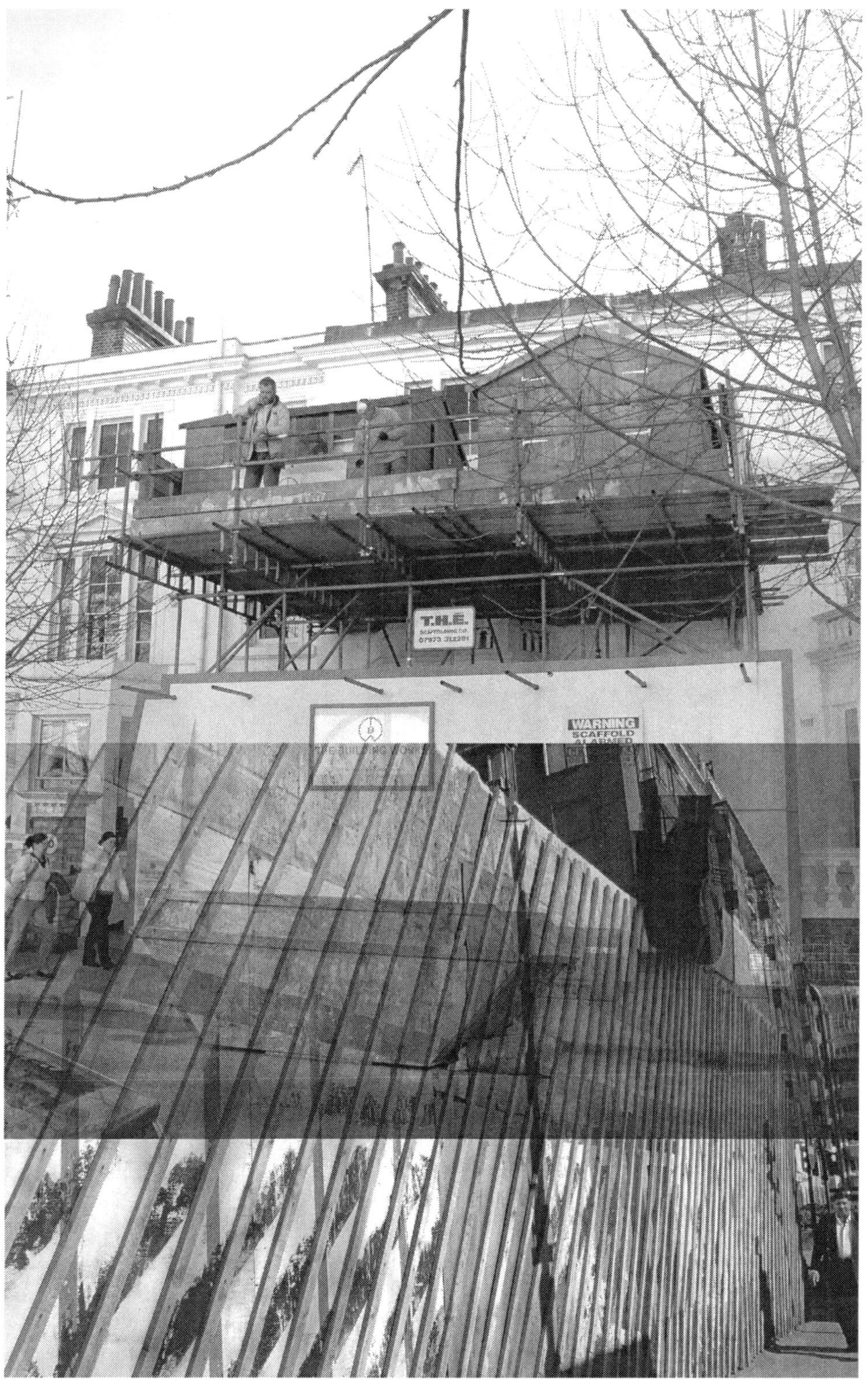
T.H.E.
SCAFFOLDING CO.
07973 312281
WARNING
SCAFFOLD
ALARMED

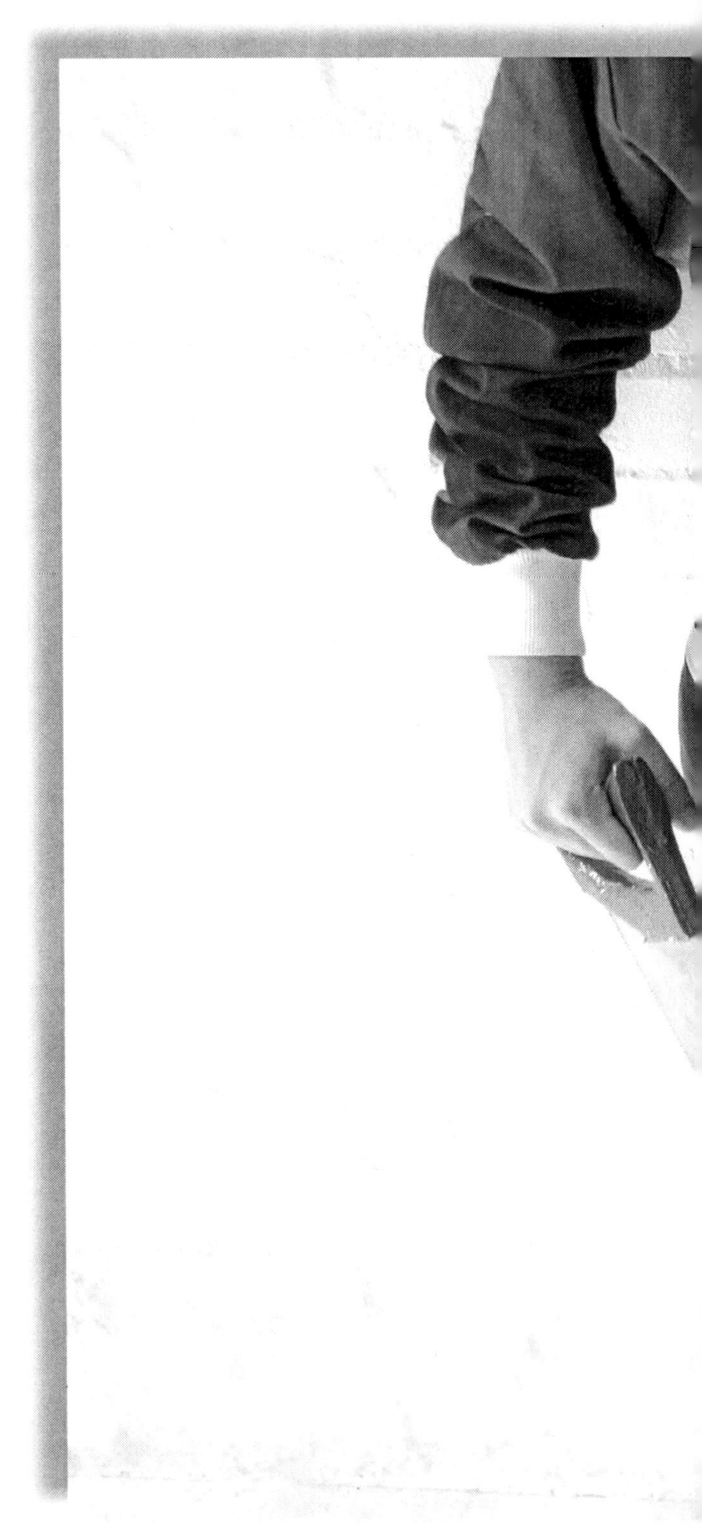

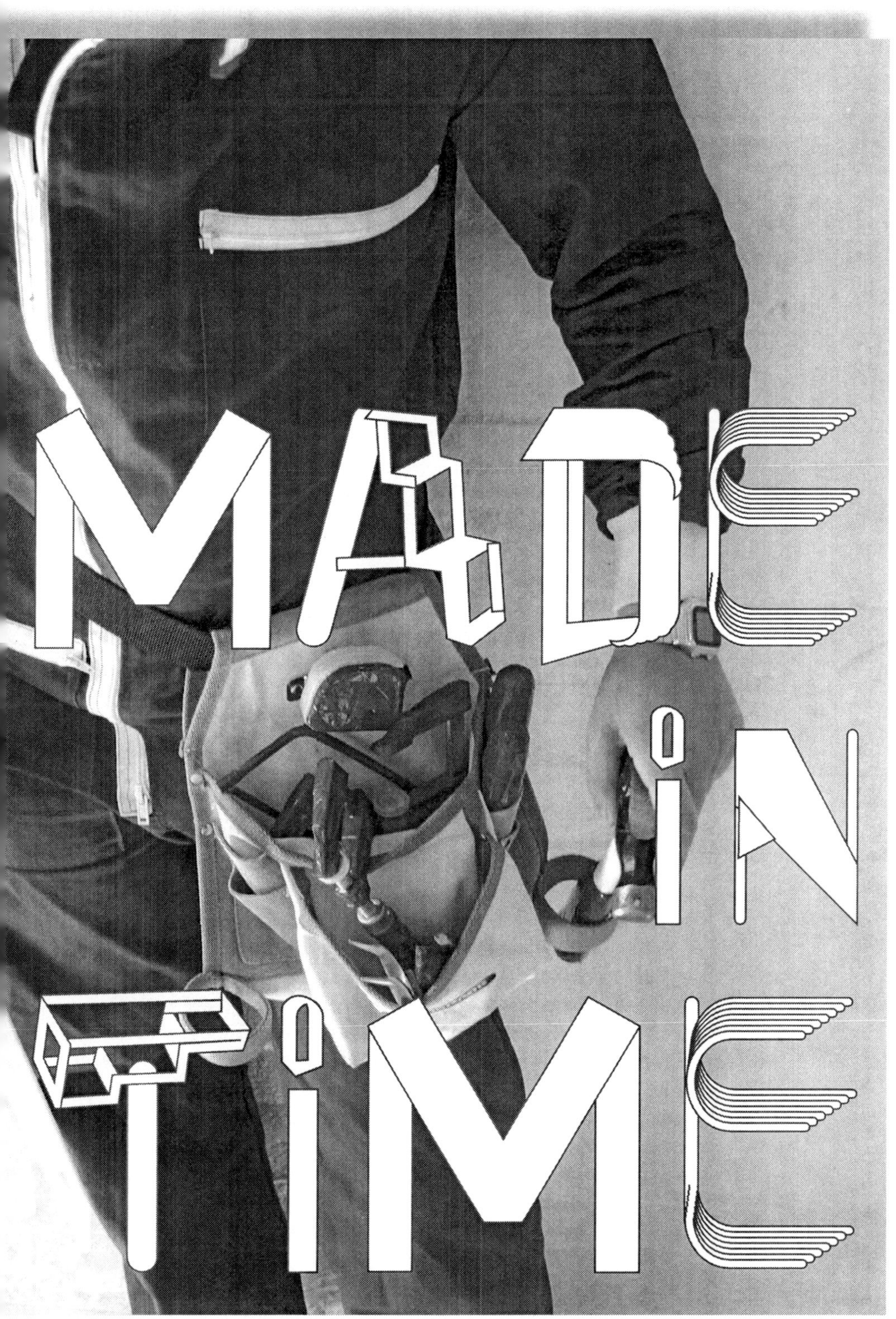
MADE
IN
TIME

MADE IN TIME

The "Made in Time" project is a performance piece. There is the worktable, the tools, the material, the prebuilt elements and the builder, which together create a scene that produces an object: a stool.

"Made in Time" is about designing the desire to get an object, to create this moment of desire with the performance. It is about how much of an object you really see, including its construction and the person who actually builds it for you on demand. It is always the same stool which is always built following the same plan, the same process, a performance running against time.

When I started this project I had different timing, short periods and long ones. It was about the quality of an object that increases with the time I spent building it. But in my experience of the performance, the show aspect has become much more important than the quality of the object itself.

The elements used for construction are highly industrial: soft, factory-cut wood and industrial covering tape. There is a conflict of techniques: the prepared industrial elements with craft-based way of working.

It is a performance that takes place very occasionally for a special event. Just at this moment, the stools are built on demand and the stool can disappear just as fast as it appeared… in 8 minutes. What makes the project is the design of the setting, the elements, the way the performance happens with the simplicity of the idea: to build on demand a stool in a short time for a short lifespan. The excitement of the moment is more important than the physical object that will most likely disappear fast because of its poor quality.

April 2008

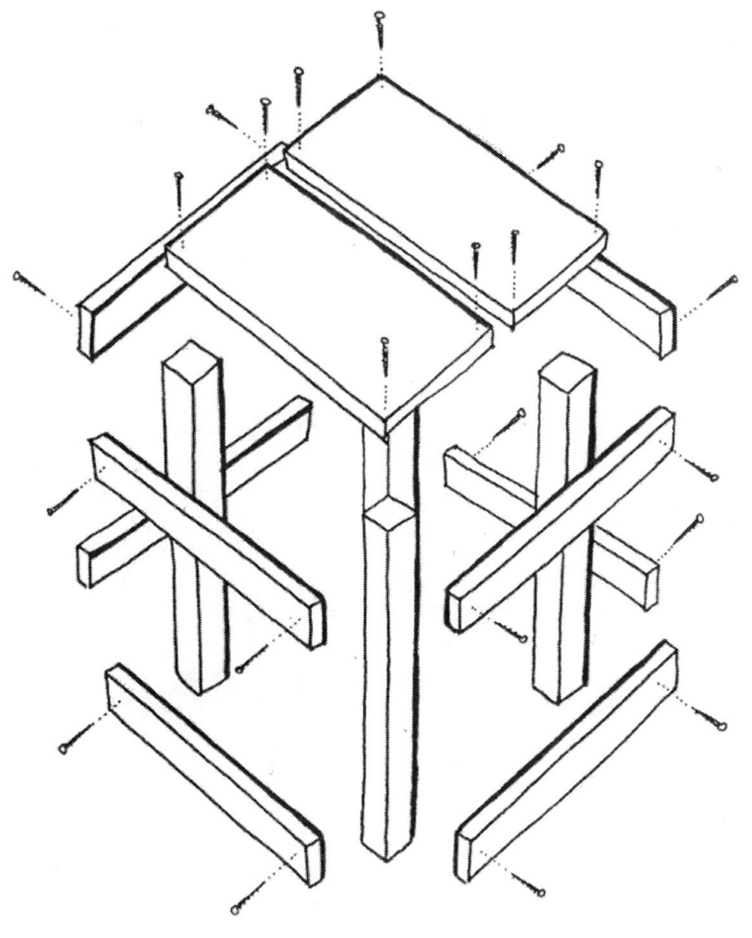

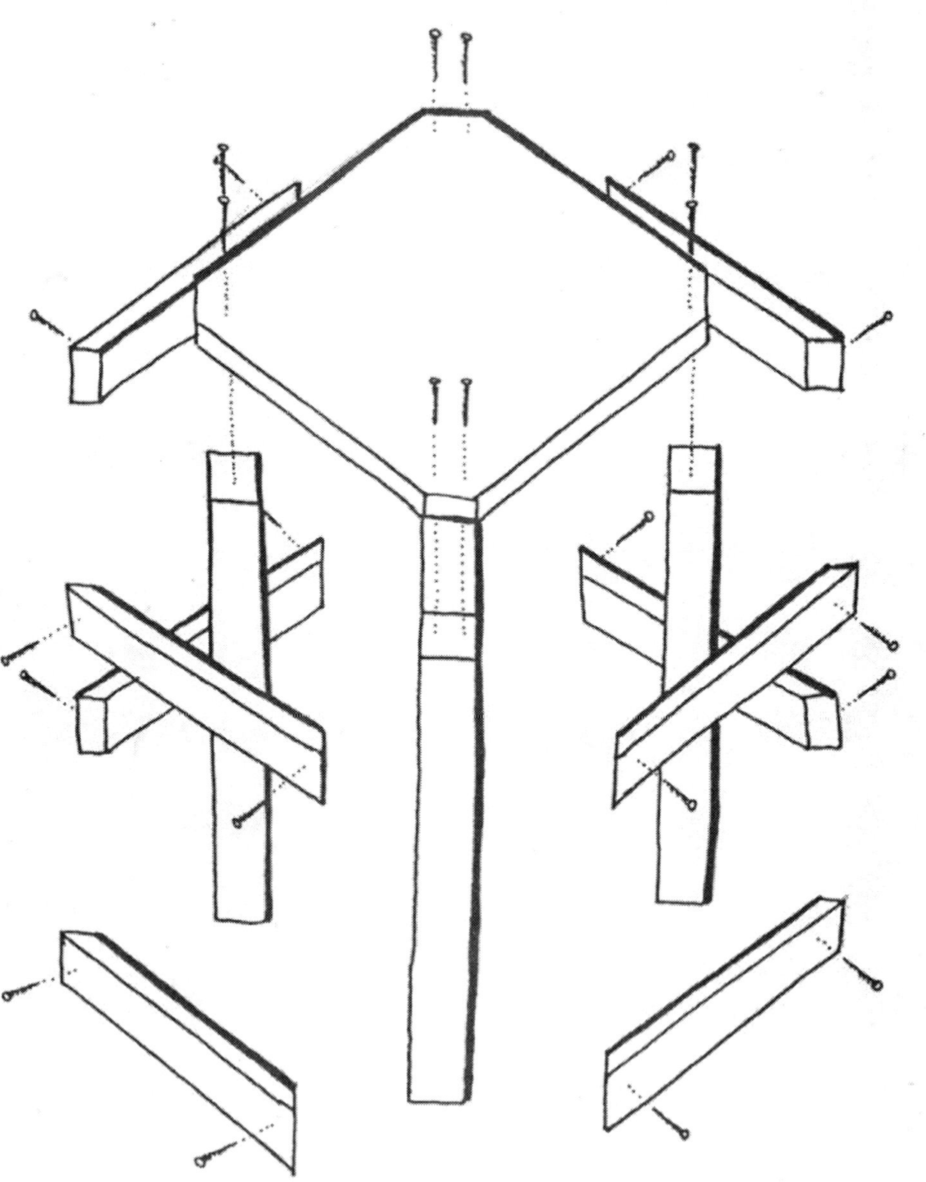

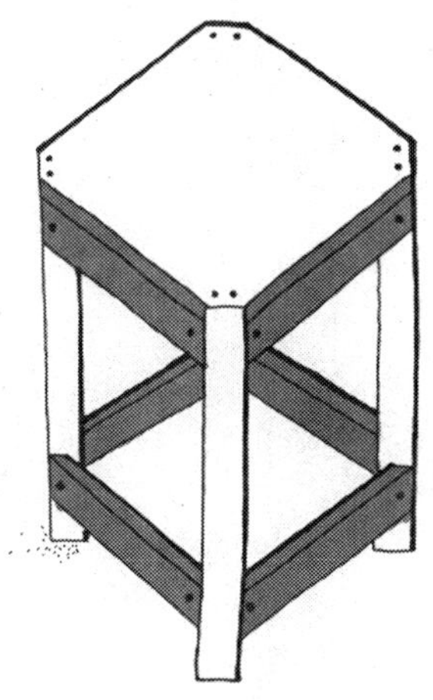

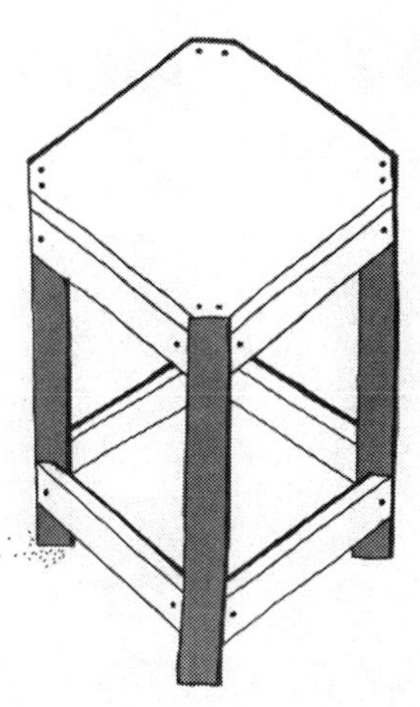

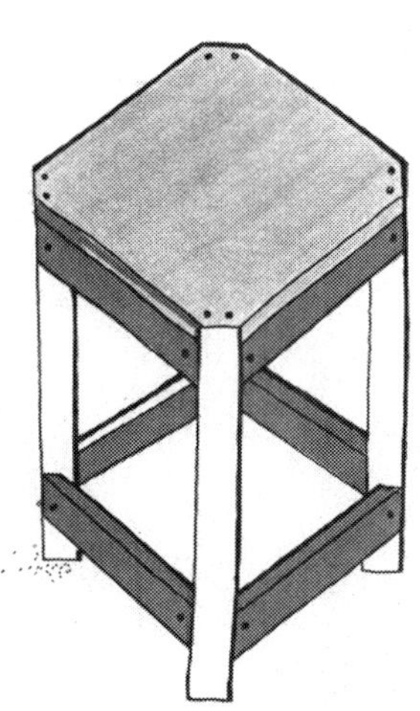

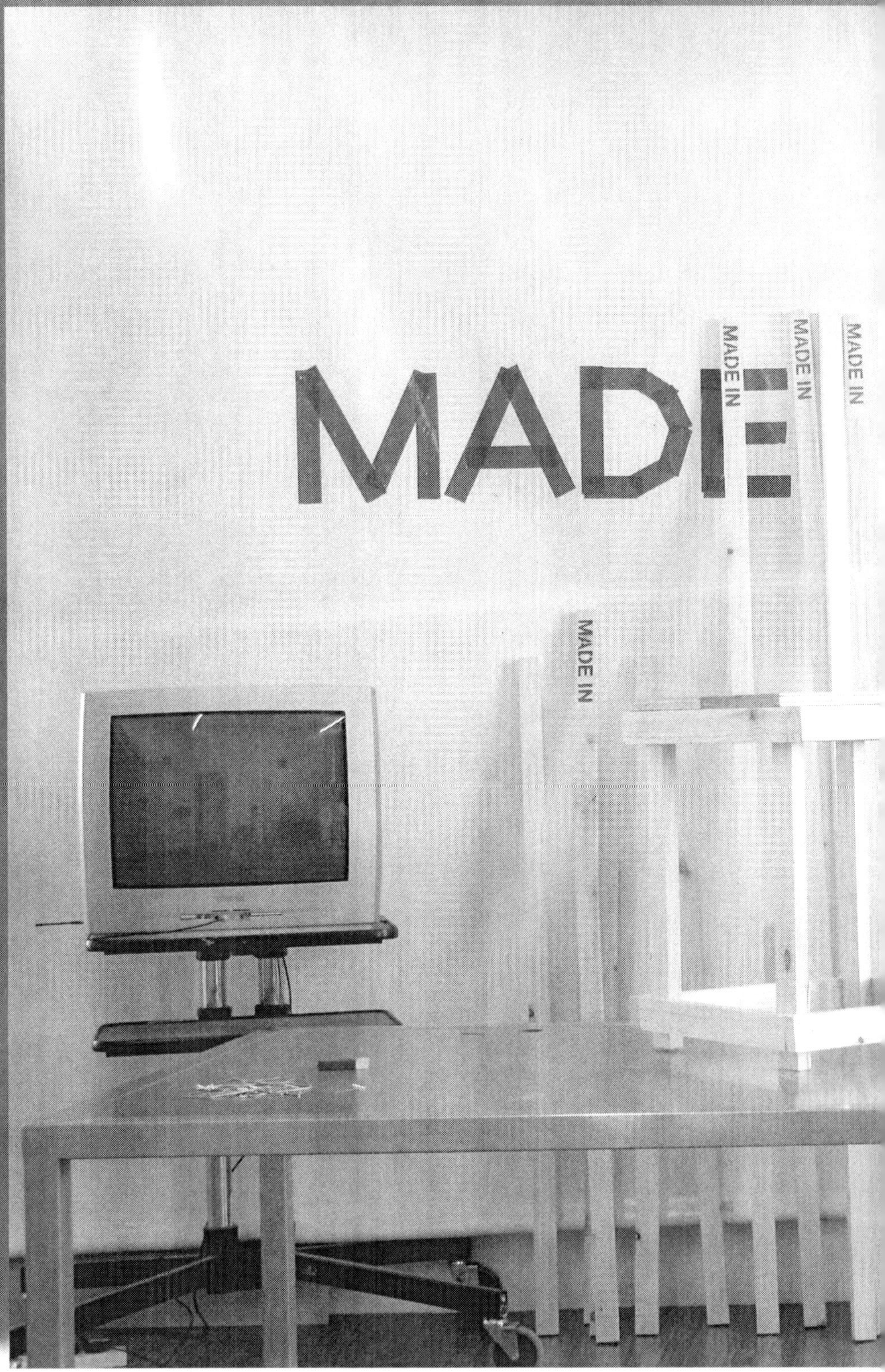

MADE
MADE IN
MADE IN
MADE IN
MADE IN
MADE IN

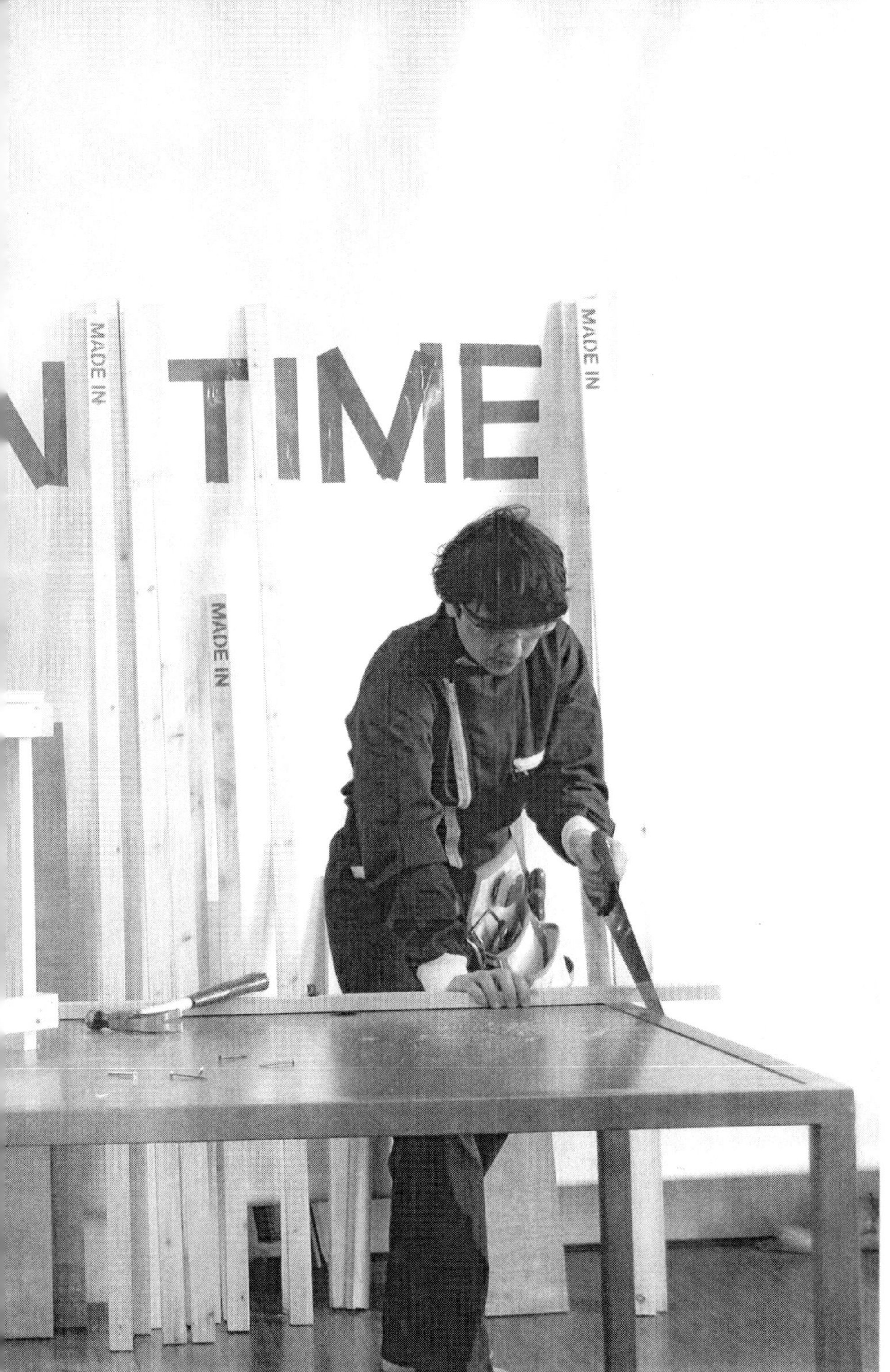
TIME
MADE IN
MADE IN
MADE IN

THE DRAUGHTMAN'S CONTRACT

There was a tree in the garden that the Emperor liked a lot. He called the most respected draughtsman of the kingdom to draw it. Everyday the Emperor visited the draughtsman to ask him if he was done with his work, and the artist endlessly answered to wait a bit more. The Emperor waited impatiently until the draughtsman came to announce he was finally ready. The draughtsman took a seat and drew the tree from memory in three minutes. The Emperor became angry to have waited for so long, realizing the draughtsman could draw it in a moment. To this he answered: 'To draw the tree in front of you in three minutes, I needed a long time of observation and practice'.

April 2007

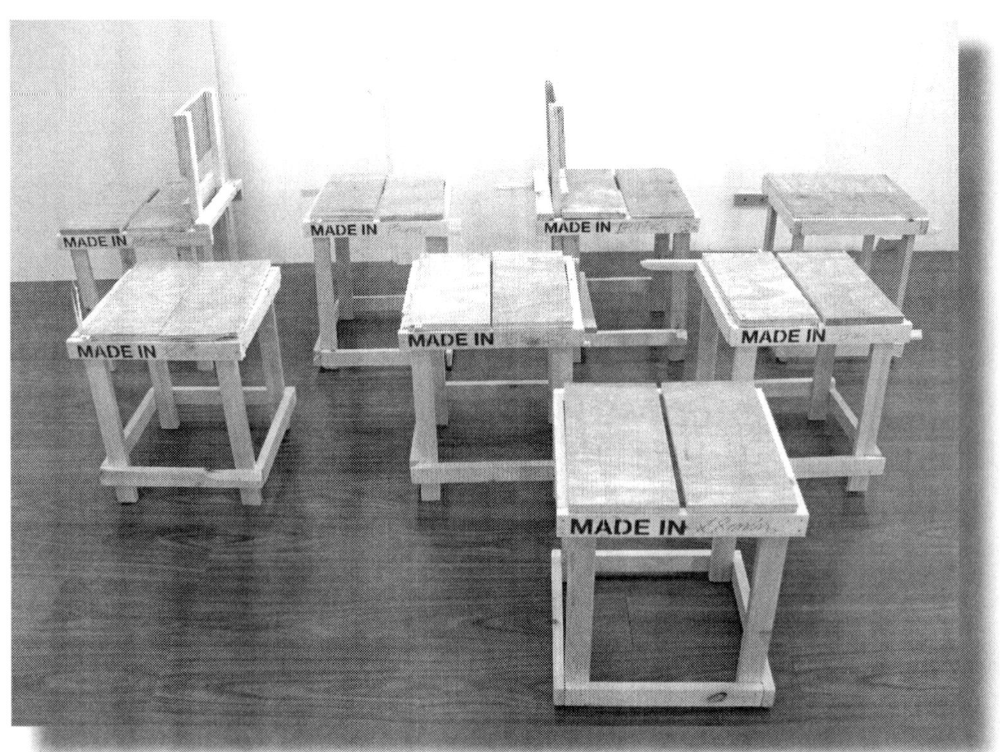

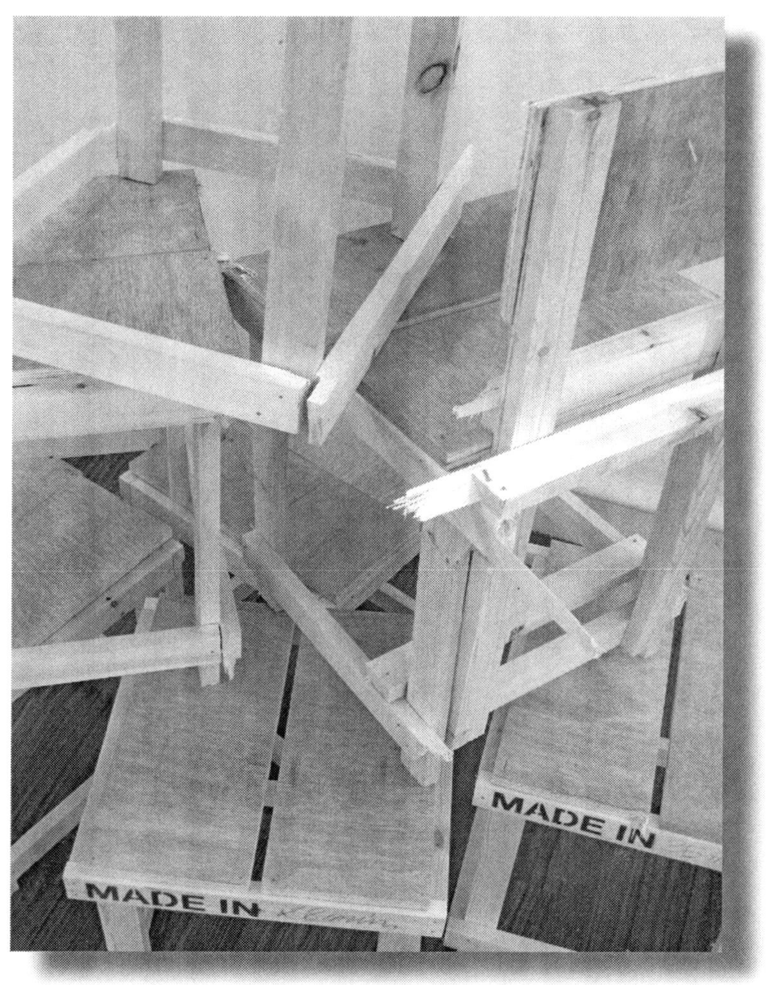
MADE IN
MADE IN

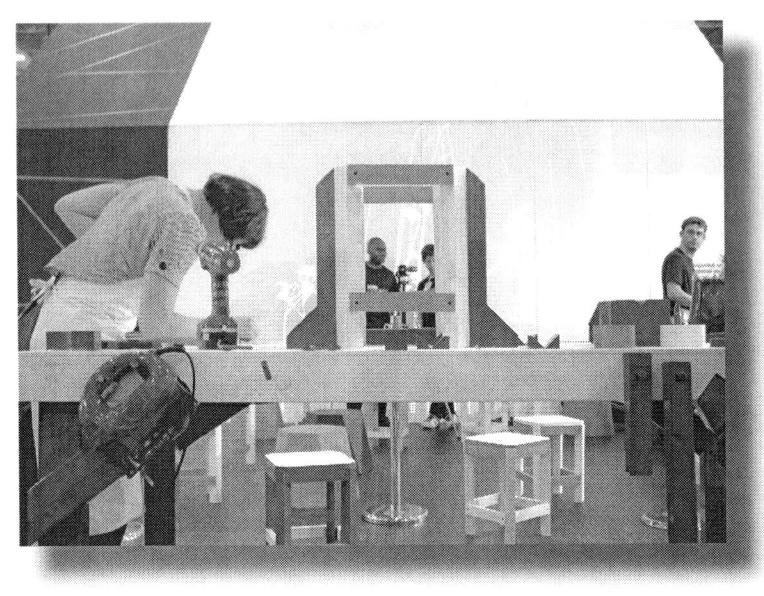

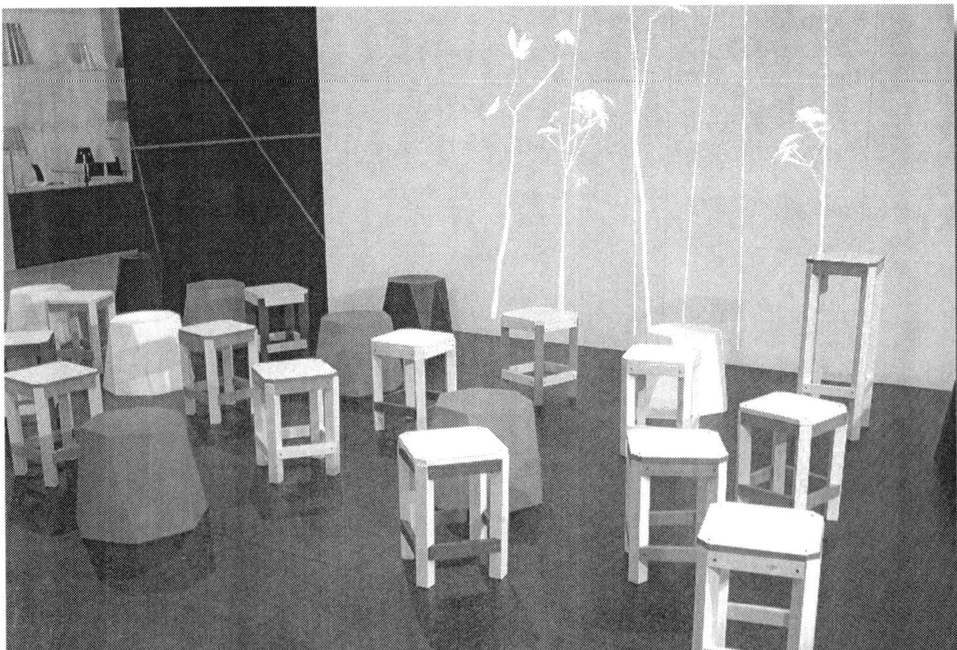

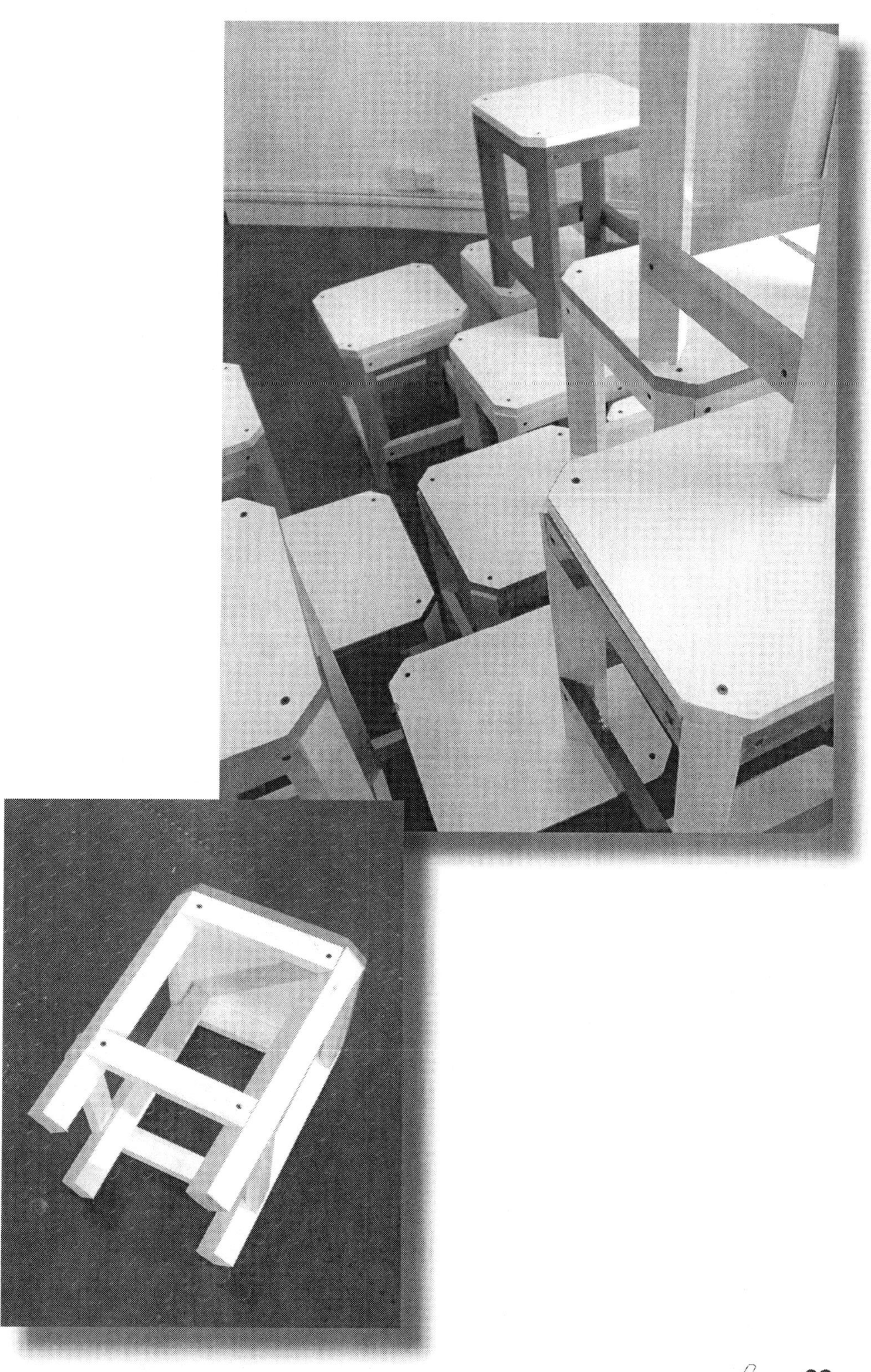

BORROW PRIVACY AND PROPERTY

The mechanisms of home answer to codes linked to the notions of privacy and property. What creates the unique aspect of each universal mechanism? There are some codes in the physical appearance as well as in the human behaviours relating to home which exist in opposition to the codes of public spaces.

To question the notions of privacy and property necessarily involves the exploration of antonyms. What makes for specificity of public spaces and sharing, spaces of non-privacy and non-property? I am interested in the meeting point of those two areas clashing, when the border is ambiguous, when the codes are confounded and the places no longer clearly identified.

The hotel room - a place where privacy and property are borrowed for limited time, represents in a condensed scene the ambiguity of having a private parcel in the city. The hotel room is a compact home exposed to the city, or rather it is exposed to the citizen in the sense that anyone can 'borrow' the same experience in the same place. But is a night at the hotel necessarily a lonely experience that takes place at one point? Here is an opportunity to confront the codes of private space and of public space, as there is also an opportunity to question the necessity of privacy and the necessity of sharing.

January 2008

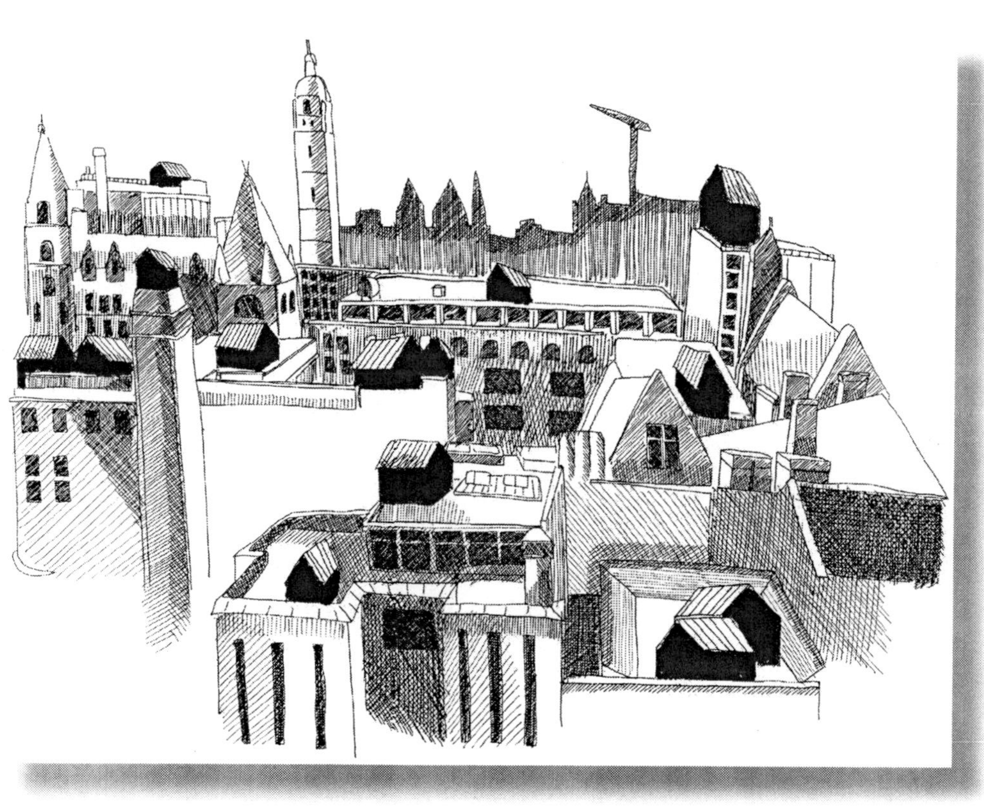

MADE TO SLEEP

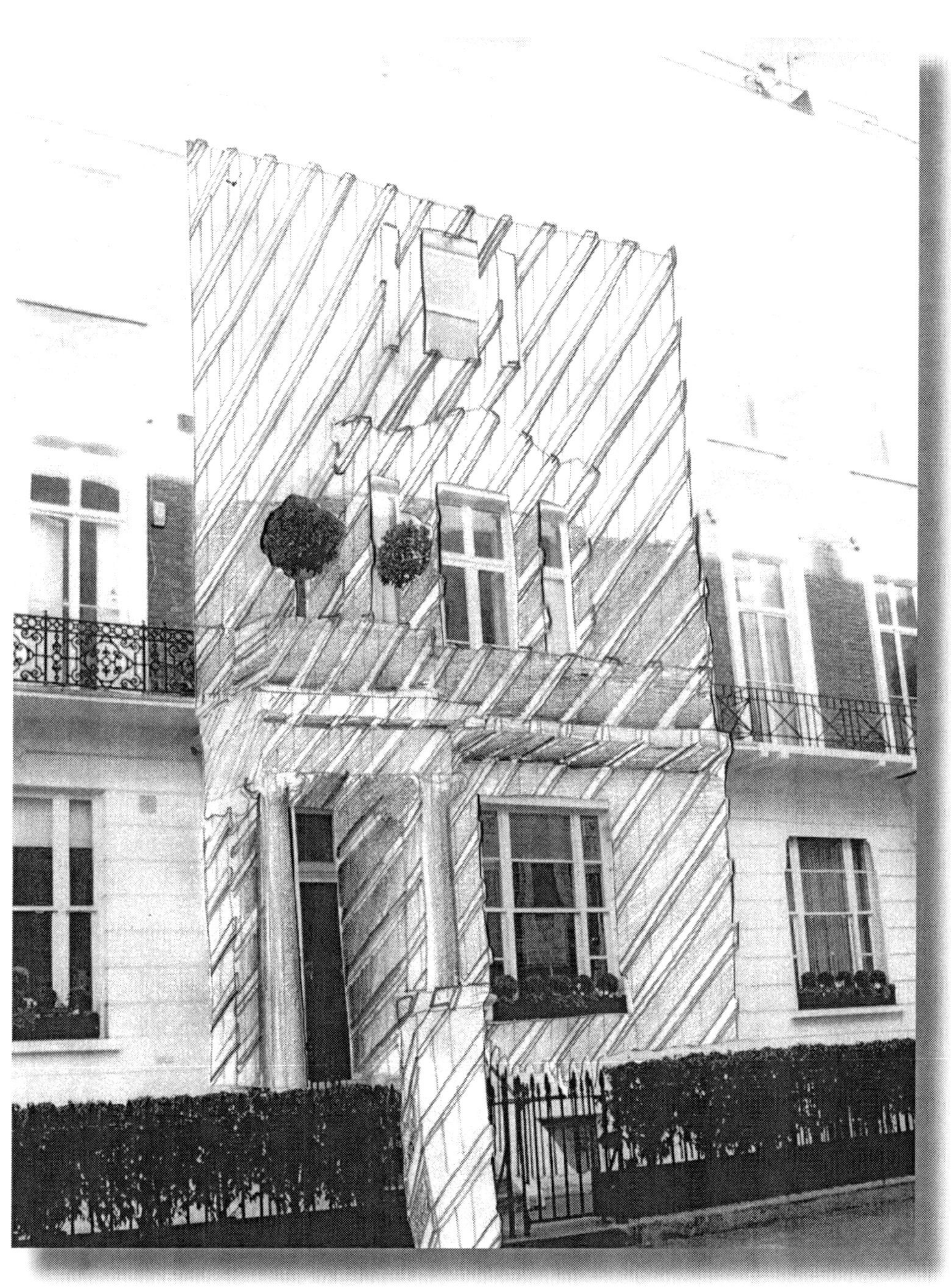

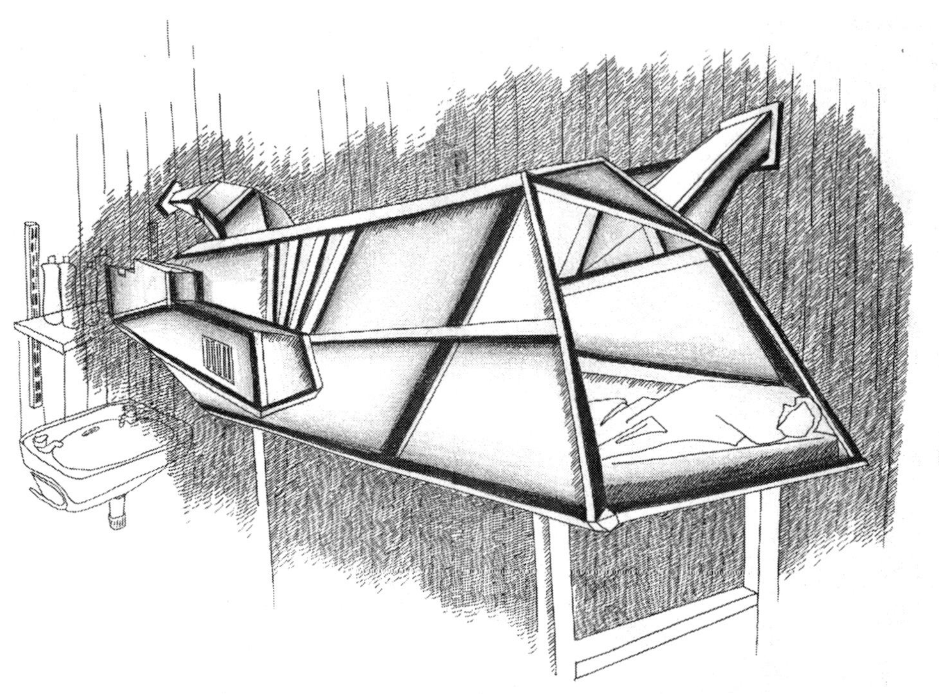

TEMPORARY OCCUPATION

The student decides to take residence in the abandoned hair-dressing salon on 33 Thurloe Street. The building is occupied once again.

The student decides to sleep in the depilation room. A functional layer is added and a sleeping pod is built.

"Made to Sleep" stands there for one week of use before having to be destroyed. It answers to a direct need for an instant use. There is an existing space around which the left-over signs of previous activity can be seen. From this space, I will build the 'under-space' that is adequate for the present use we want from it. I am using the surroundings to make design decisions: like using the massage table for the bed element, or isolating the general lighting of the room to drag into the sleeping unit. The material used, the formal language and the way of building relate to hoarding techniques, temporary building.

February 2008

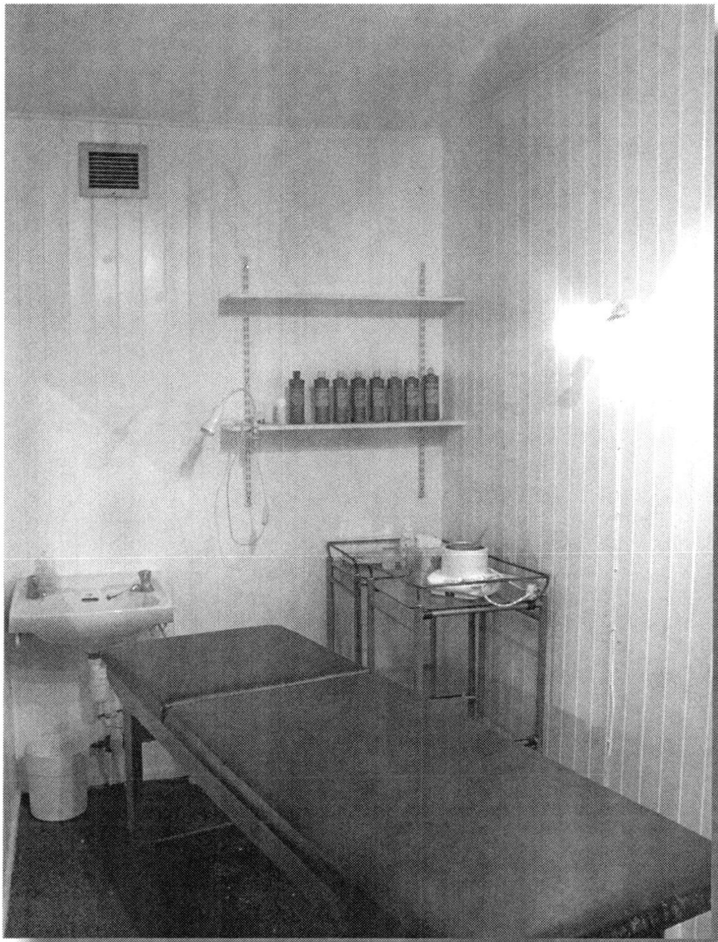

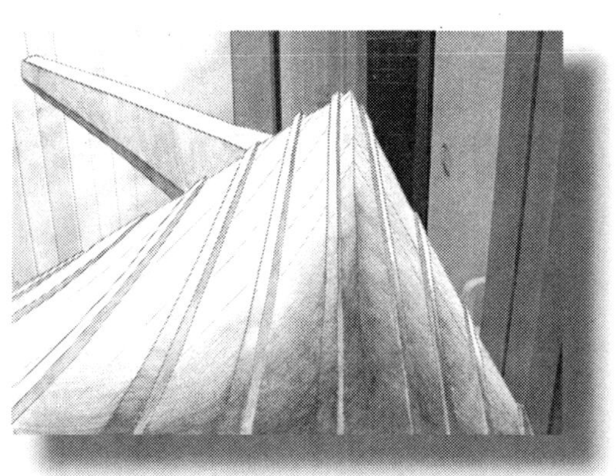

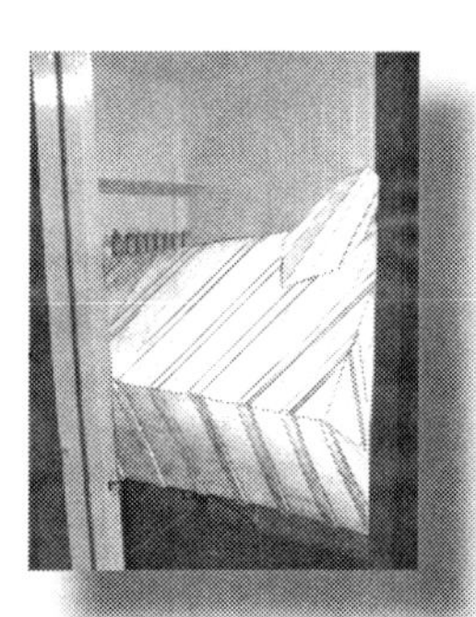

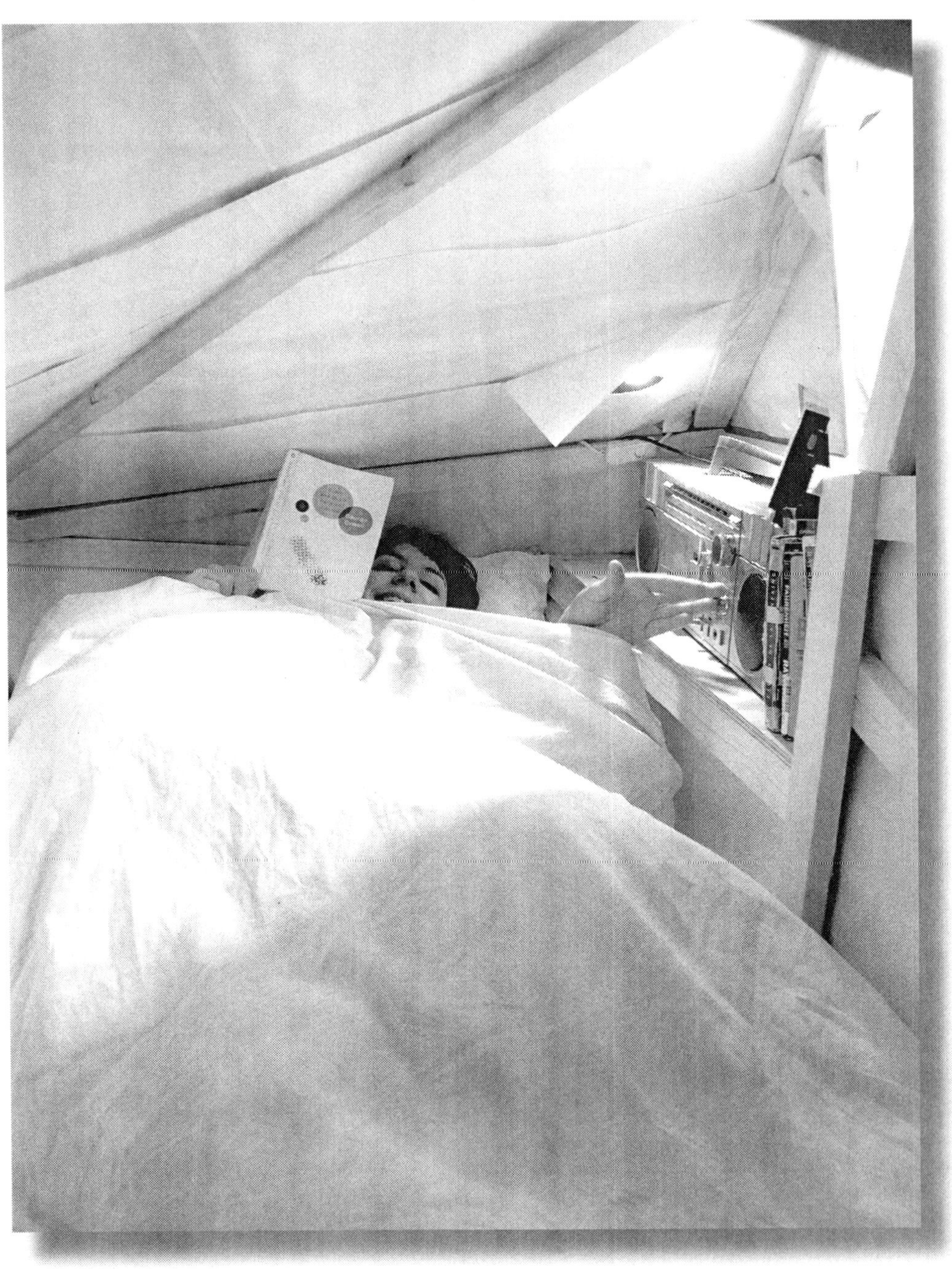

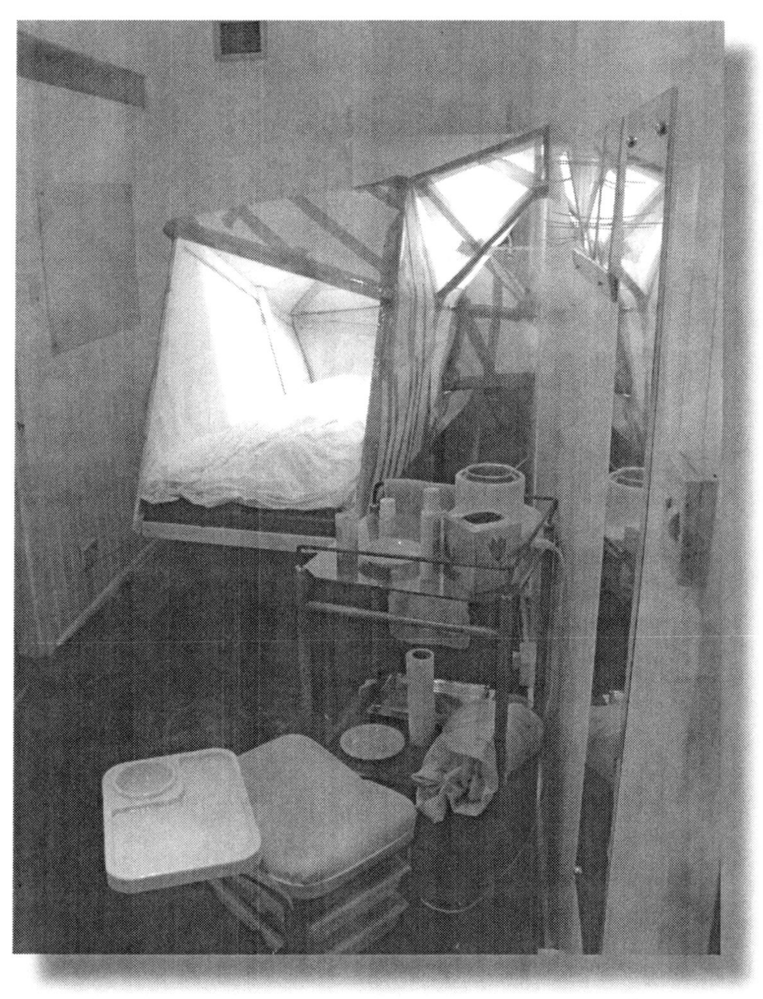

MADE TO SLEEP TWO

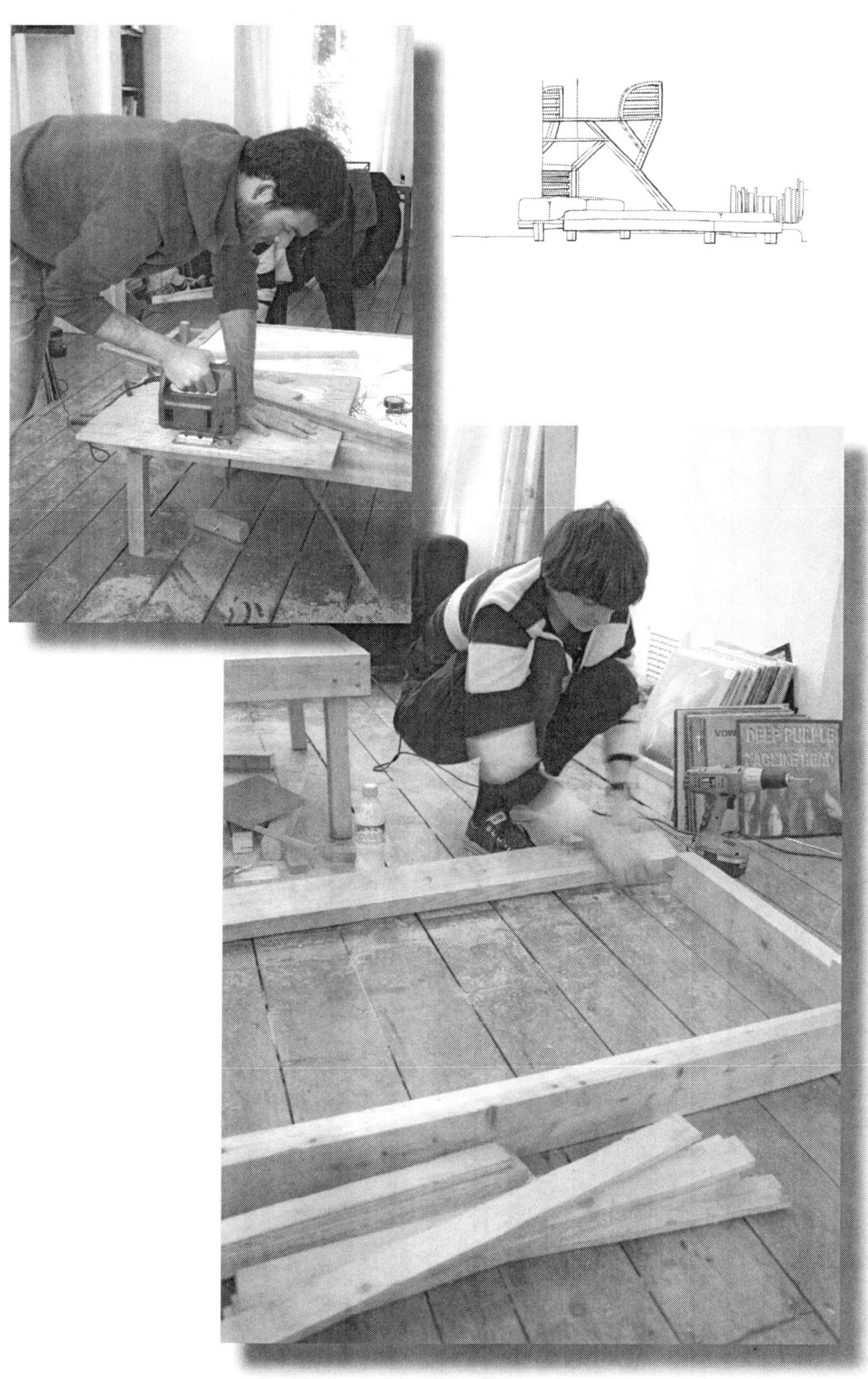

DEEP PURPLE
MACHINE HEAD

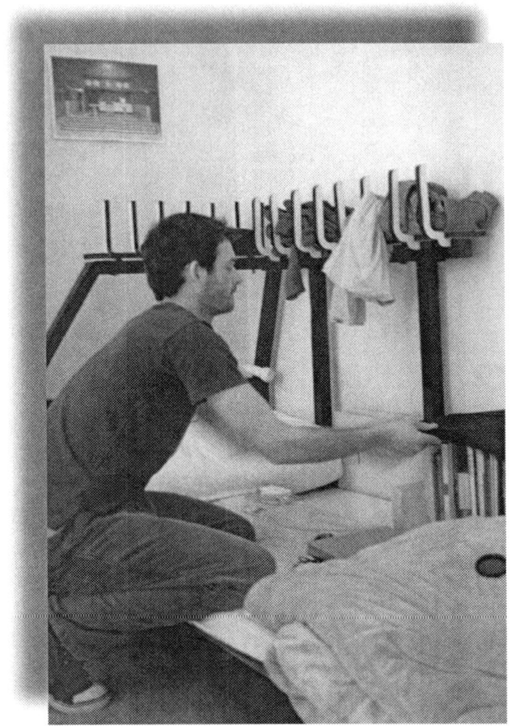

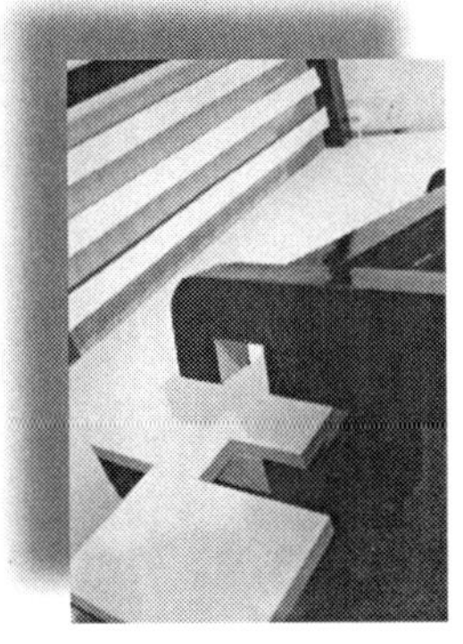

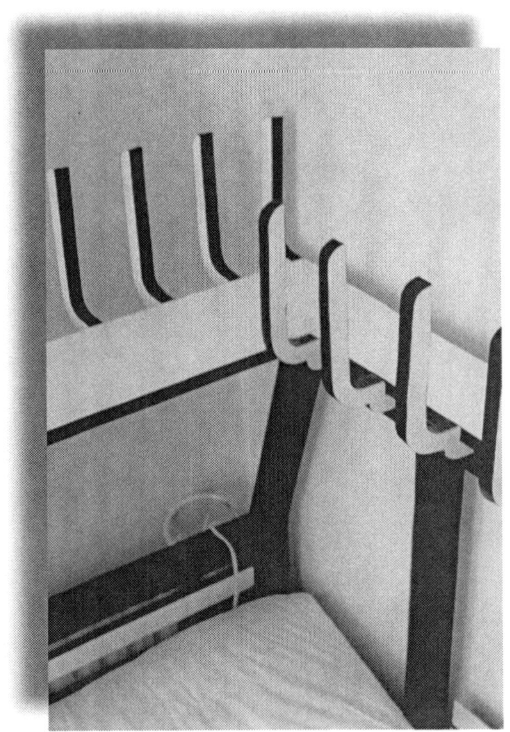

ADRIEN IS STAYING LONGER

My friend Adrien is coming to live with us. Adrien will spend five weeks at 190 Leander Road. There is no room for him but I have decided that he will have his own space inside my room. I will make a bedroom within the bedroom. The corner facing the window along the bookcase, with the radiator on the left, will be the space for his belongings and a bed. The living room will become the workshop. Adrian will help me during

the construction process. Adrien will
spend 5 weeks at 190 Leander Road.
        This is about how the situation
of designing an object, a space in the
space came to me. The whole process
belongs to one place: the drawings,
the plans, the building, the use.
When Adrien leaves, the object loses
its value. There were three things that
defined this object: the room, the
situation which brought Adrien here,
and Adrien himself. So the object
disappears or transforms itself. The
object has been partially reused for
a personal purpose, and the other
part has been used to build a sculpture,
dedicated to the memory of Adrien
living in this room.

March 2008

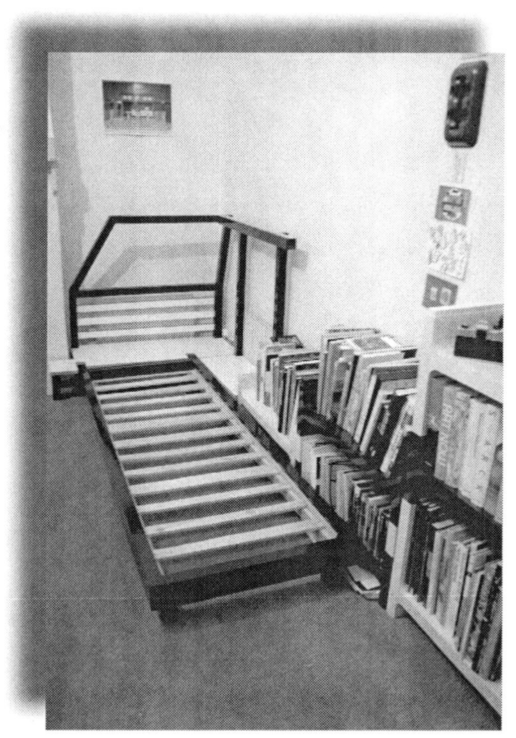

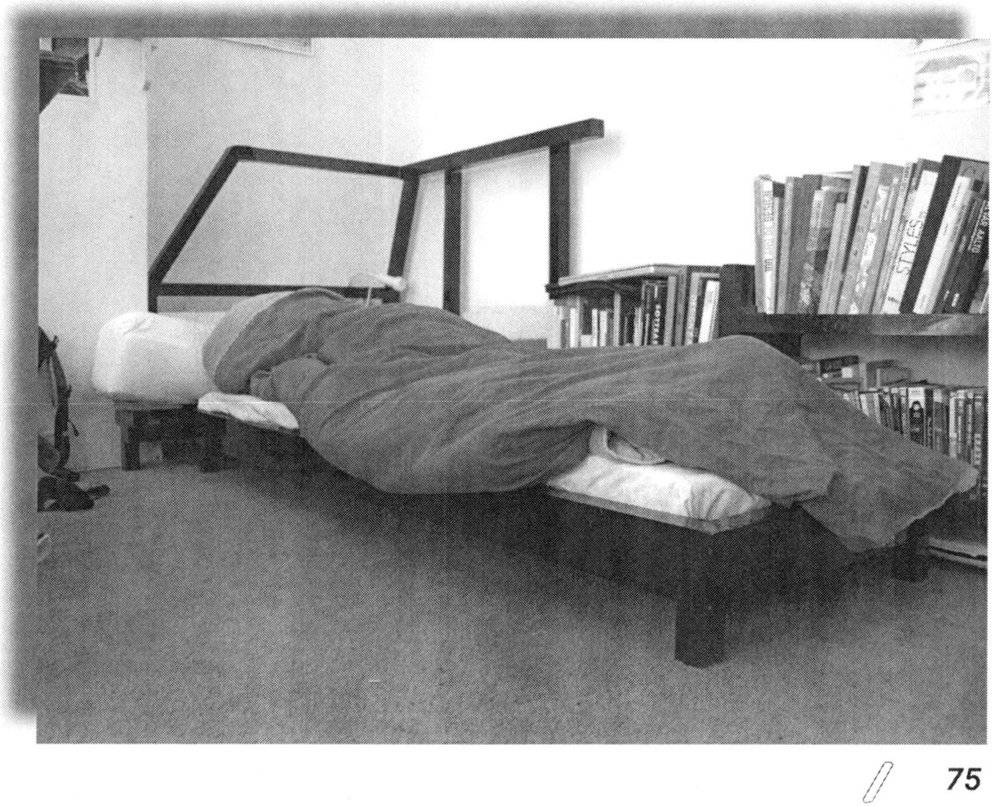

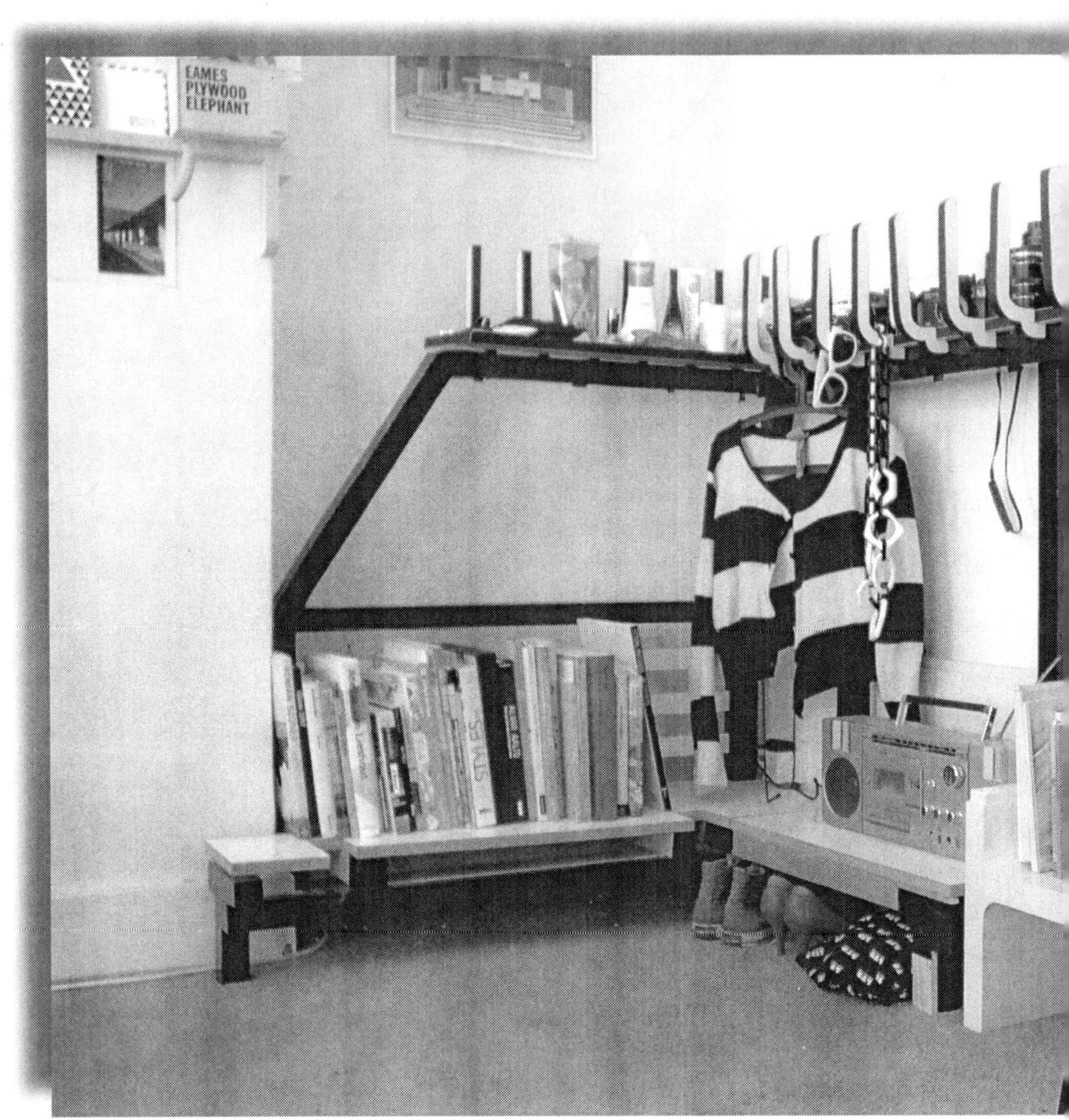

Adrien is not there anymore.

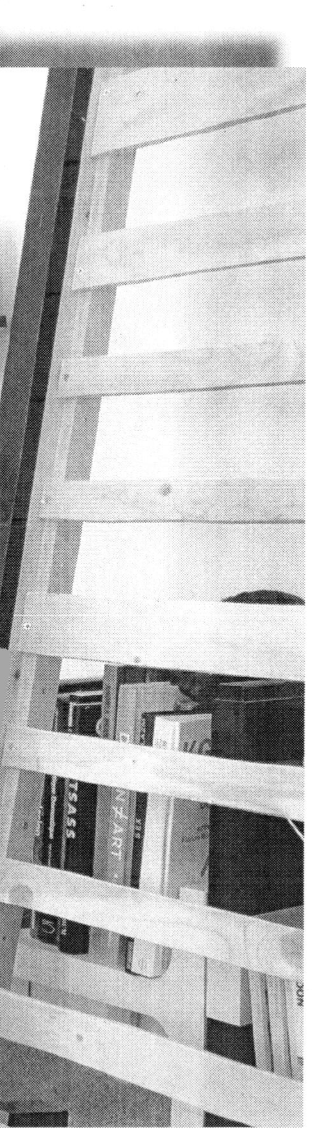

THE OBJECTS OF OUR LIVES

Modify the relationship between the objects and the environment; that means the relationship between the objects and our way of living with the objects; modify the mechanism of the space or the position that people take among objects.

The idea that objects can be close or far from us, that space can be larger or reduced. Like this, the one who live in the middle of his objects, furniture, can decide to be close or go away from them, if he wants to do so. Each one should be able to manifest the situation of his life or the one of the group with the objects, the furniture in an environment. Our objects are not the background that make our lives, the objects are the servants of the life we want to have, or the one that happens to us. We do not stick to objects, the objects stick to us. But this is without considering what Ettore Sottsass called the 'global logical system': this system which carries the idea that the "solution has been reached, to invite planetary tribes not to waste time thinking, because everything has been already carefully thought out". We need people who do not necessarily believe in the global logical system.

November 2007
Quotes from Ettore Sottsass

CITY ADDICT

A city is not made by size, job, history or architecture, but by eternal energy and a certain kind of energy which is extroverted and self-disregarding. A city's special quality is its autonomy: it goes its own way, and lets you go yours. Only if you do not like it, the city does turn this isolation into loneliness. The City would then say, has a right to say, "if you don't like me then Sod Off." The City has a right to say so because of the facilities it provides and the way in which it provides them. Only addicts need apply.

The good hotel room is, in fact, the paradigm of the city: it provides everything you really need, and no more. The rest is out there: your dining room, the city's restaurants. Your garden, the city's parks. Your transport, a bus or a taxi. In a positive way it achieves what so many societies have turned to negative effect — through commune or kibbutz — by removing the need for useless possessions. Positive, because it offers more than it takes away. Precisely because it is impersonal, it offers a secret private life as well, for the possessions which really matter. How much do you really, really need to own, continuously? Love, a sense of humour and the understanding which makes the conversation a truthful meeting instead of a conversation of blind projections; these take no room up at all. A couple of essential objects for your private comfort. The rest, the City can provide, when you want them. That is its job.

Clearly, many people want more than this. Fine: there is no lack of alternative environments. The City, if it's good enough, will achieve this without any kind of pressure. What you cannot do is have your city-cake and eat it by yourself.

The City (or the Campus) for us students is a base

to investigate and to exploit, as a training ground for applications of our projects; it is the opportunity to apply all the thoughts developed and collected at college. The college cannot afford the necessary confrontations for the expansion of the project. I call the Academy that keeps its knowledge for itself the "masturbation room." The doubt is comfortable, it is warm and pleasant. Insecure grounds are outside our knowledge. The Academy cannot afford this necessary confrontation for the expansion of the project. The luxury of study is ultimately time, the time to go deep into something as with any skill. The Campus is where our citizen's lives take place. We have to feed the "city-cake" and make it richer in order that it feeds us well in return.

February 2008

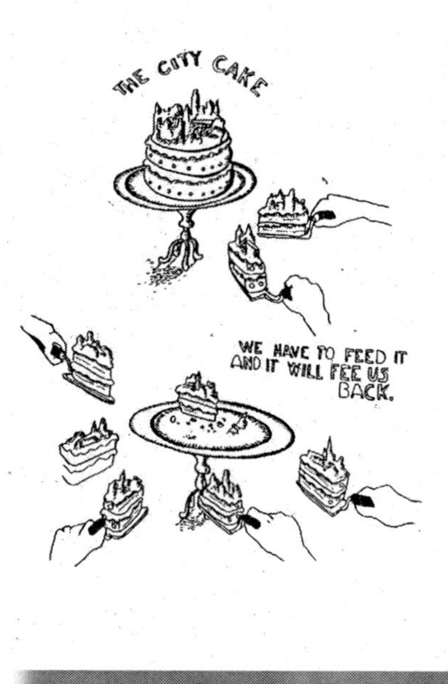

MADE FOR LOOKS

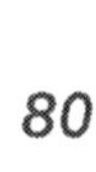

80

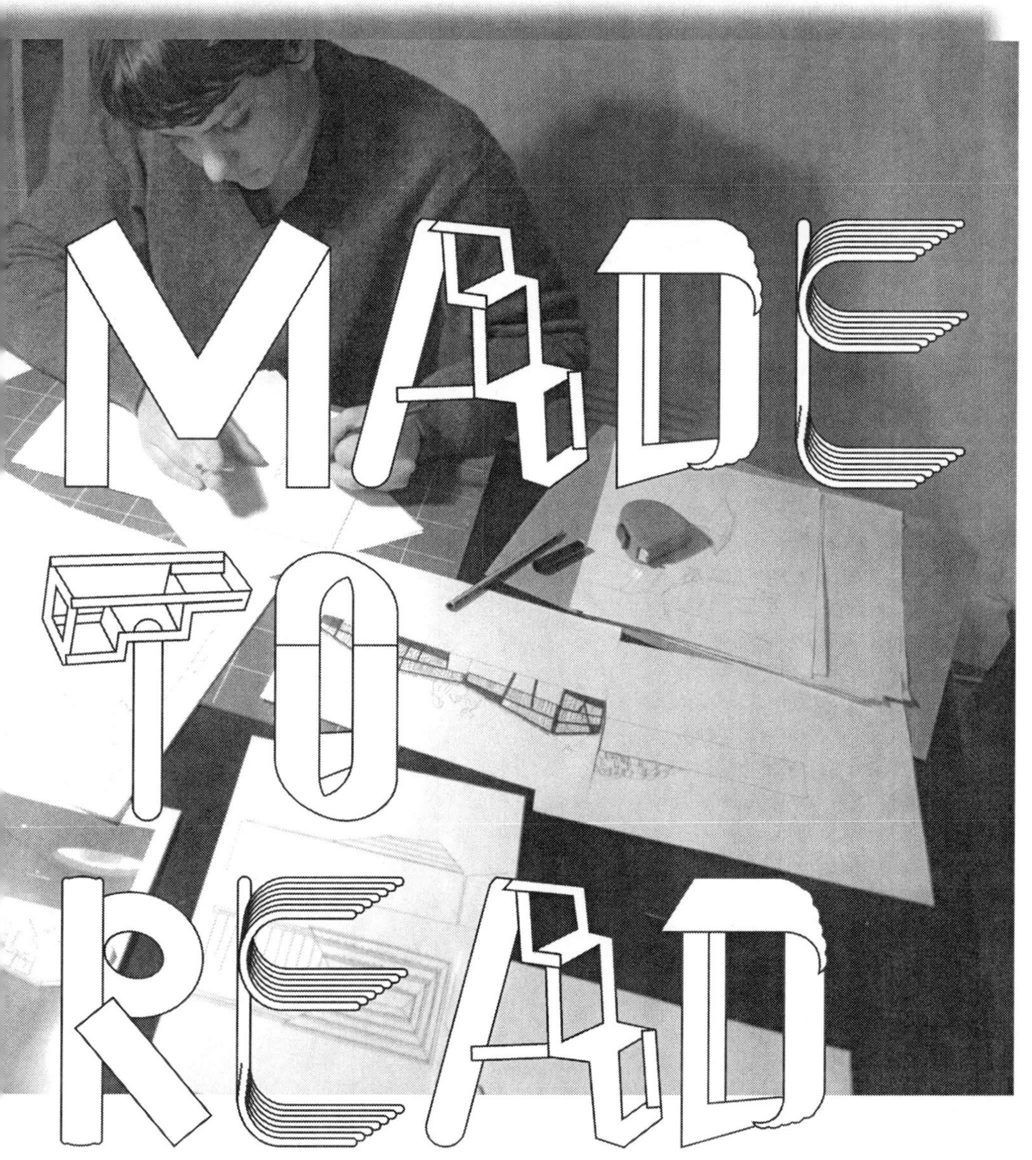

MADE
TO
READ

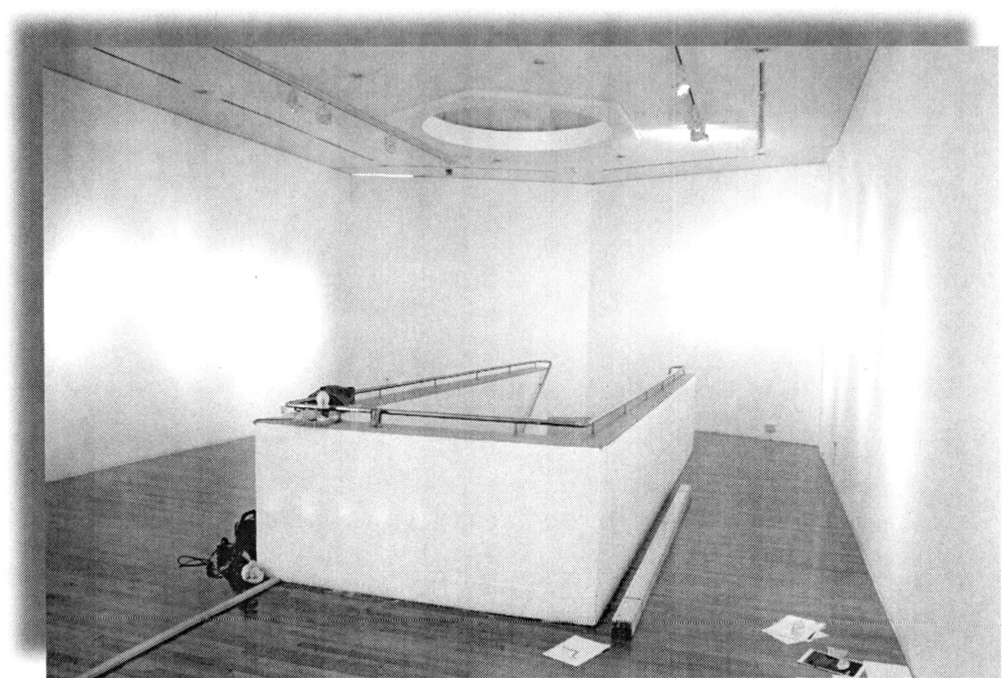

BOOKSHOP

These two spaces have been built on demand for the Curating Departments final exhibition. They formed part of a 10 day site specific installation. After that, the work is destroyed. Some elements have been kept for the building of another space...

This is a process that starts to be constituted. The design and the building of spaces into other existing spaces happens simultaneously. The drawings are made in the space, from photomontages. They provide the plan, which is not really fixed because the rapid building requires me to be flexible enough to make corrections in the space. The bookshop and the reading area have been physically developed within 9 days. The materials in use allow me an easy manipulation of the forms which shape the entire space using the existing surroundings as a mould for details. After these 10 days of use, the activities for which the installation have been built disappear, and so do the objects. The spaces are destroyed. Nothing happens. A temporary event, a temporary activity and need, a temporary building.

April 2008

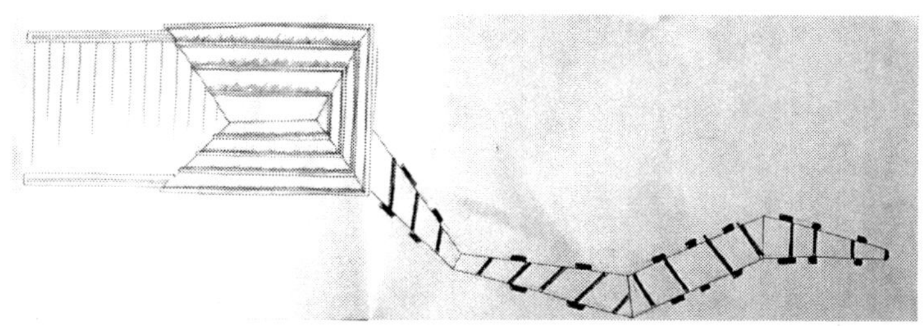

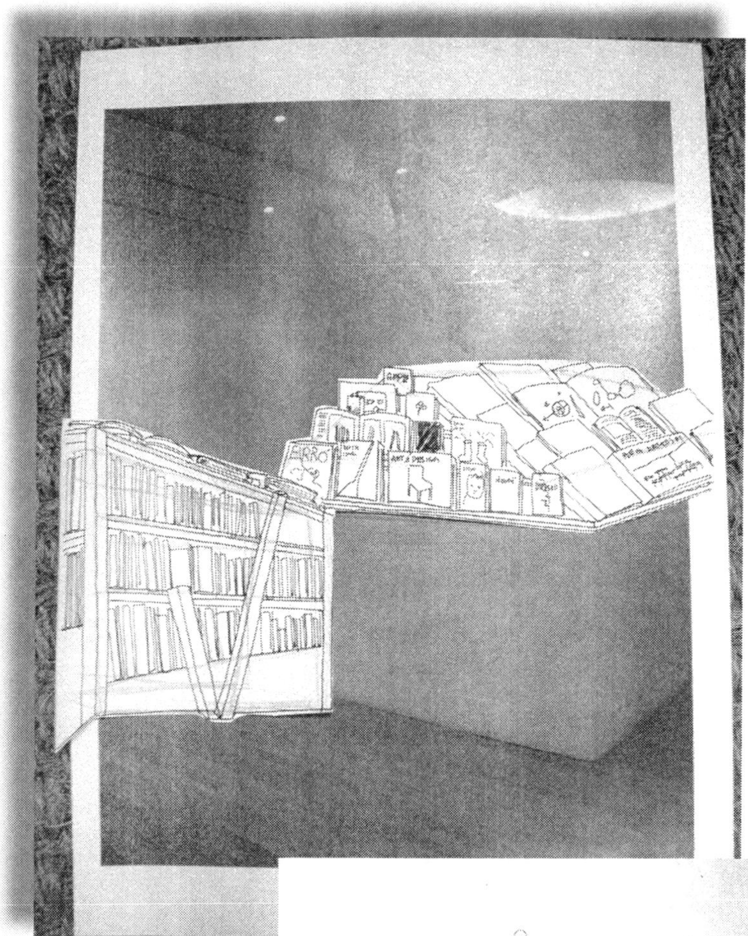

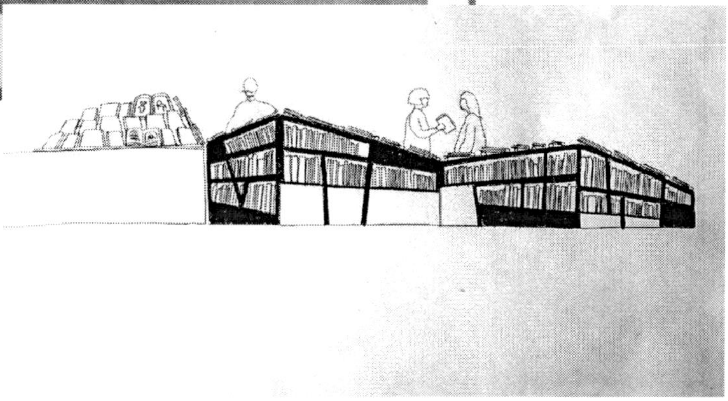

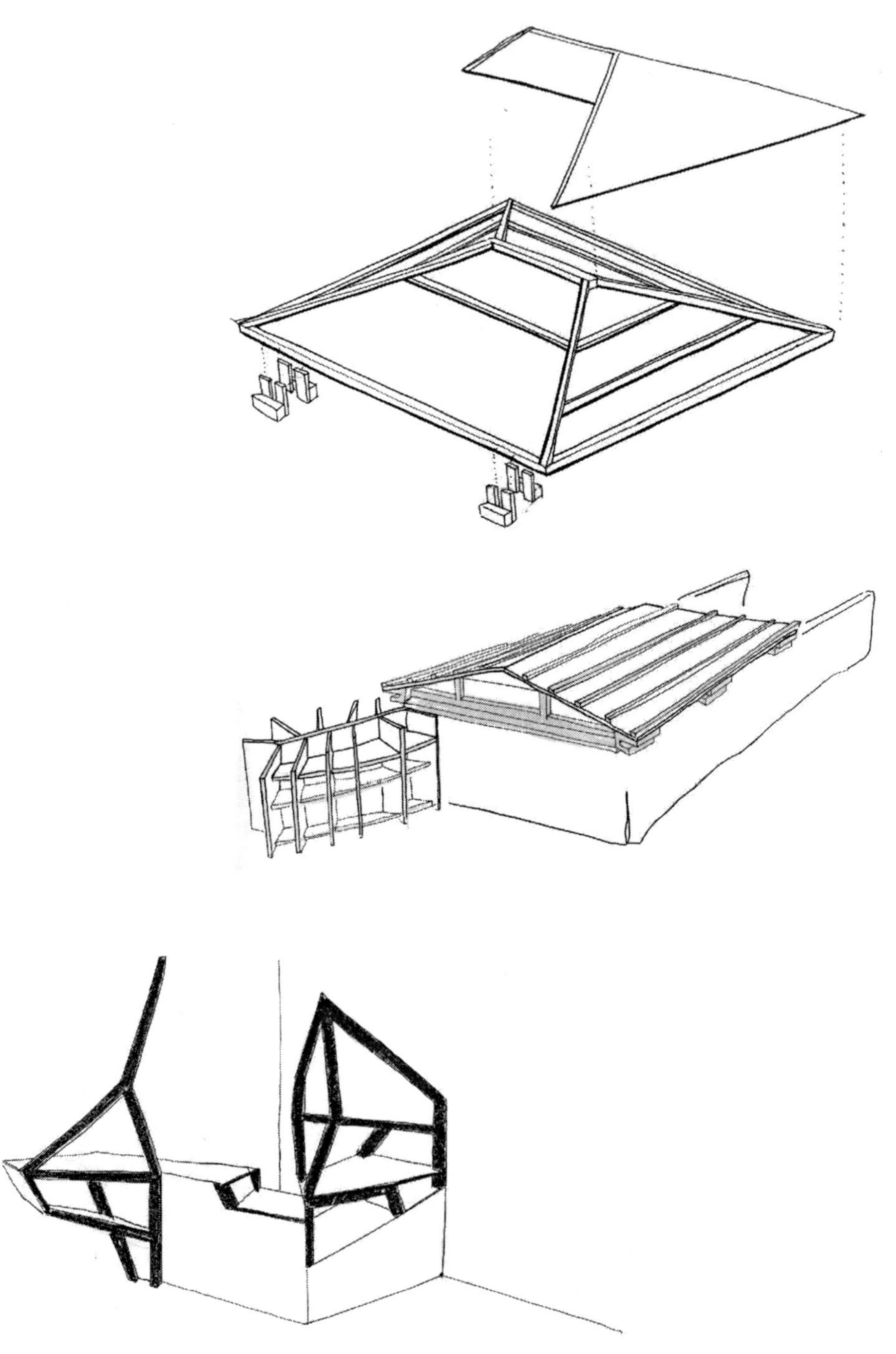

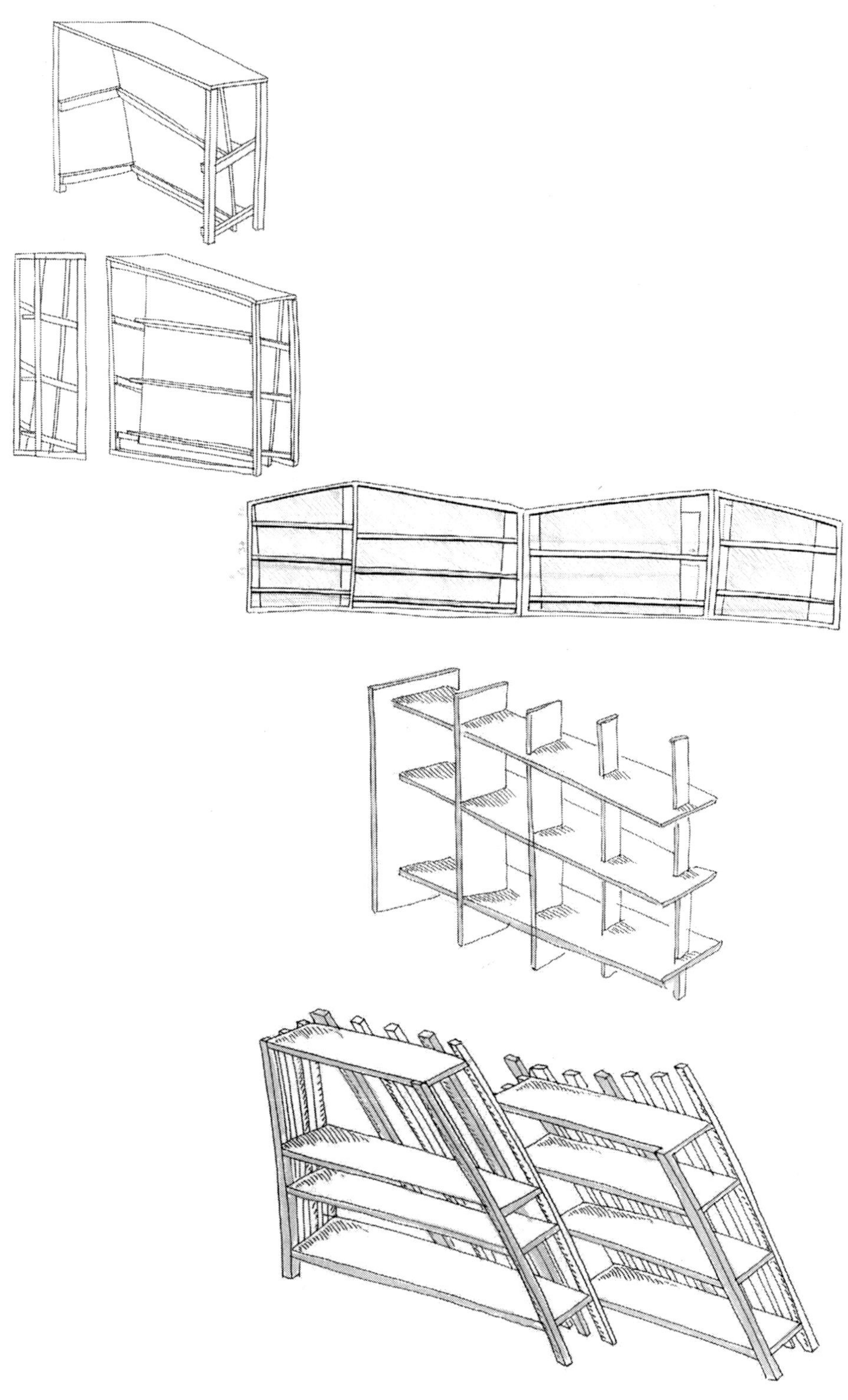

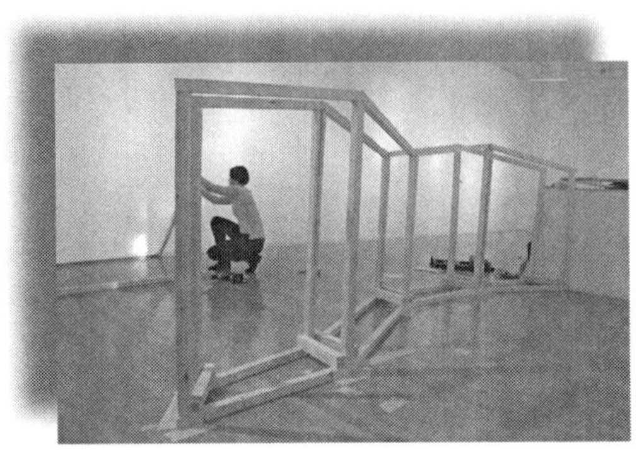

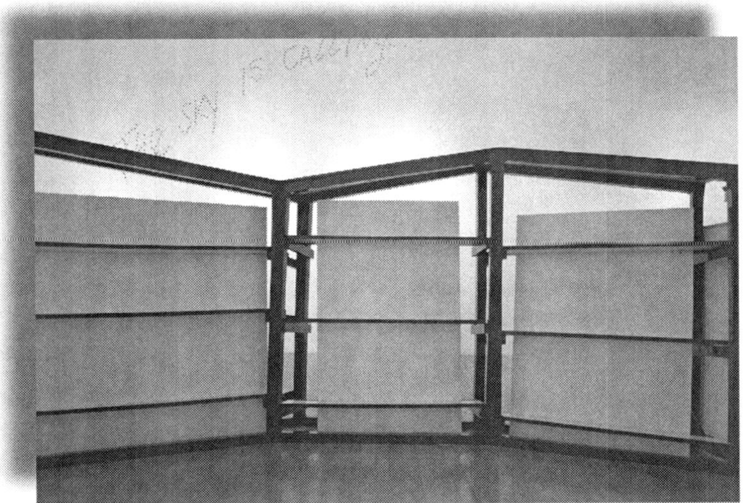

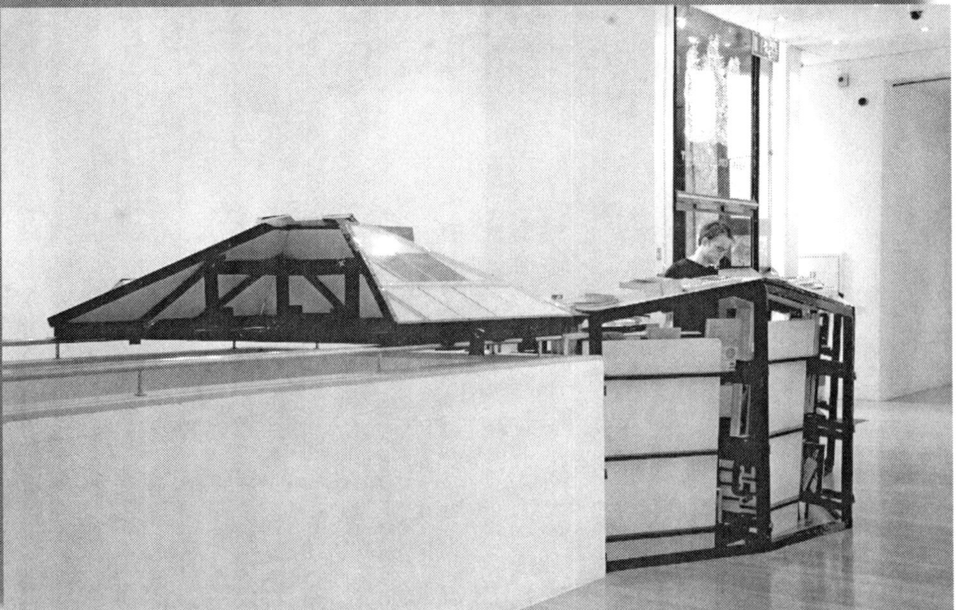

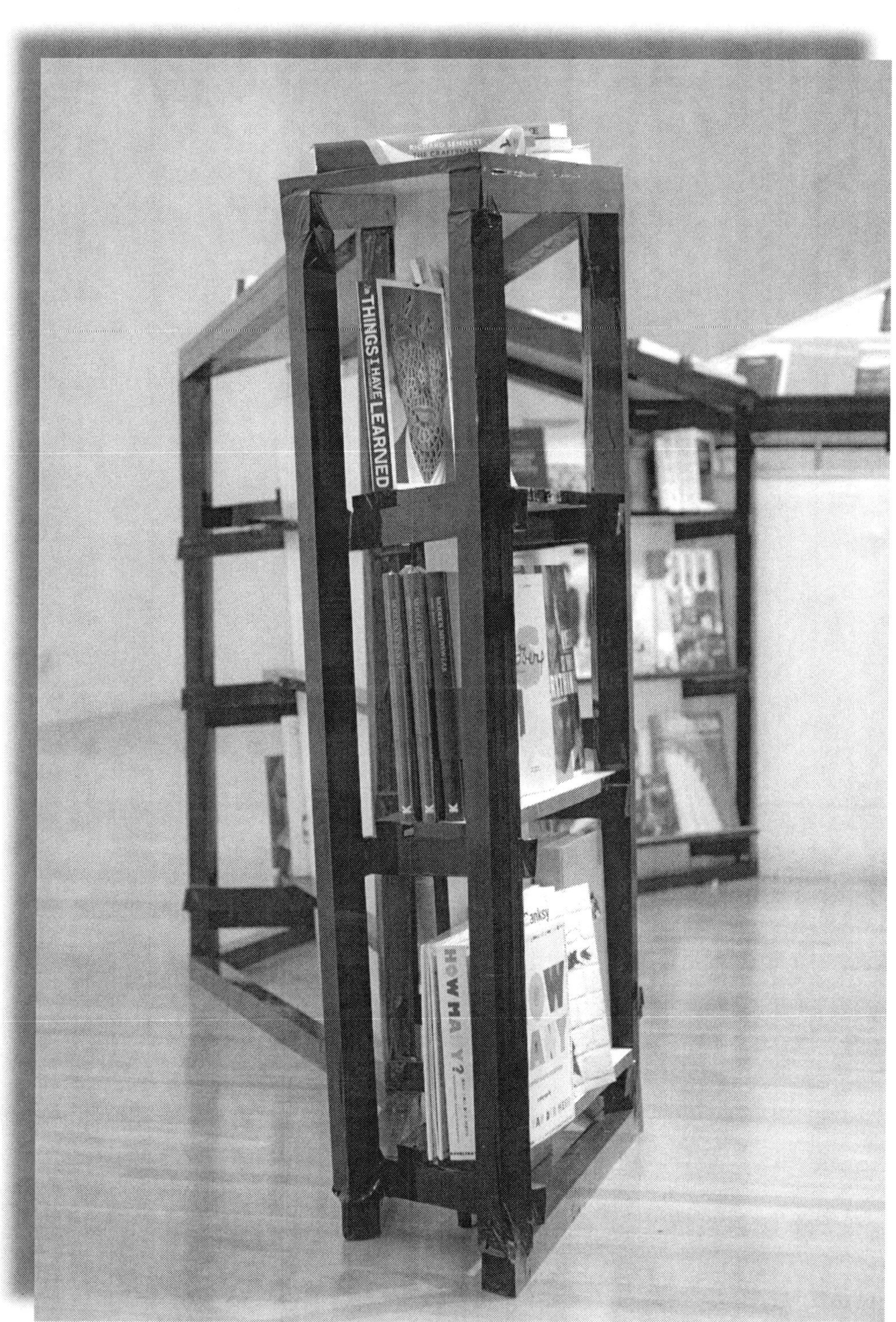

THINGS I HAVE LEARNED
Banksy
HOW MA Y?

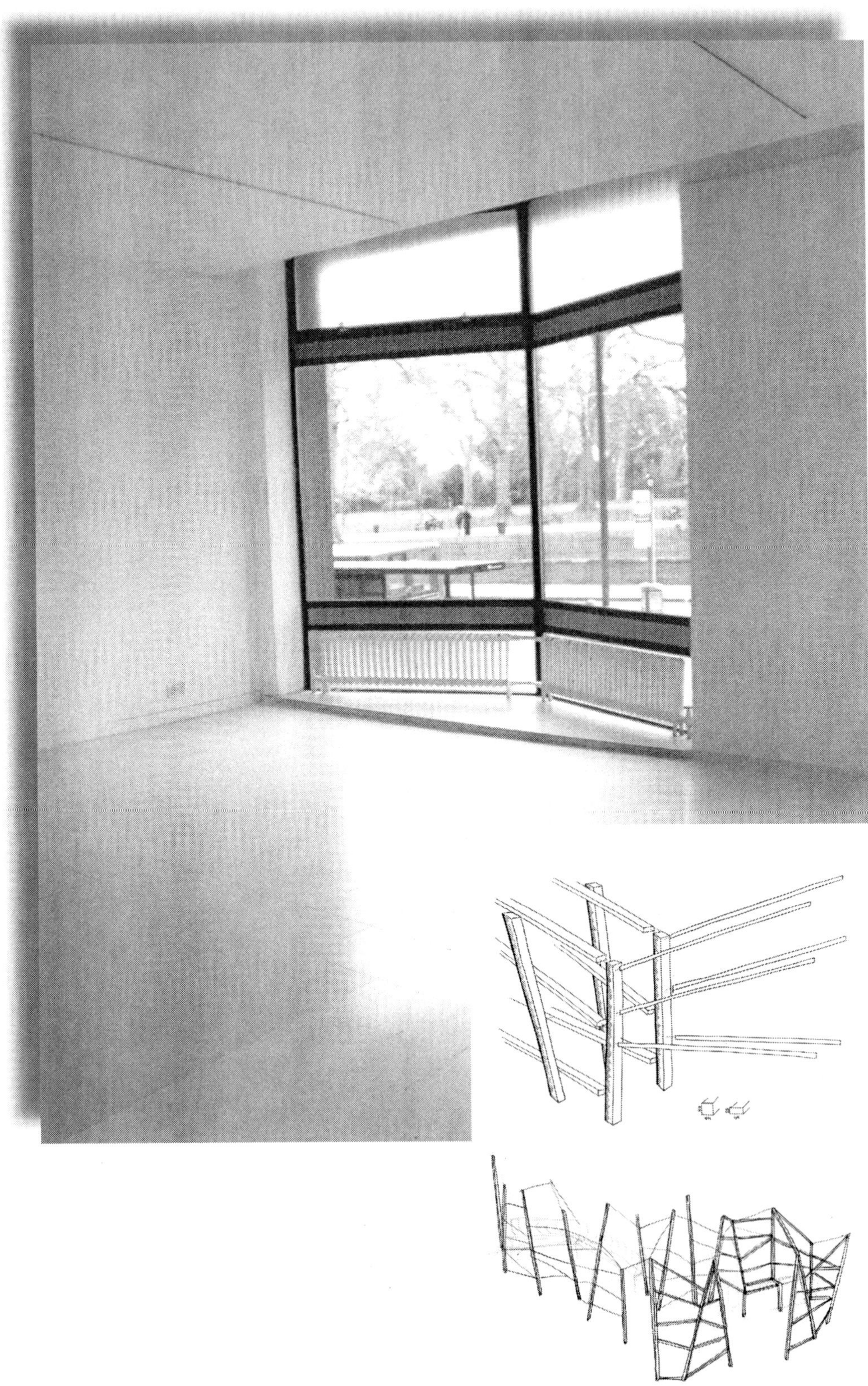

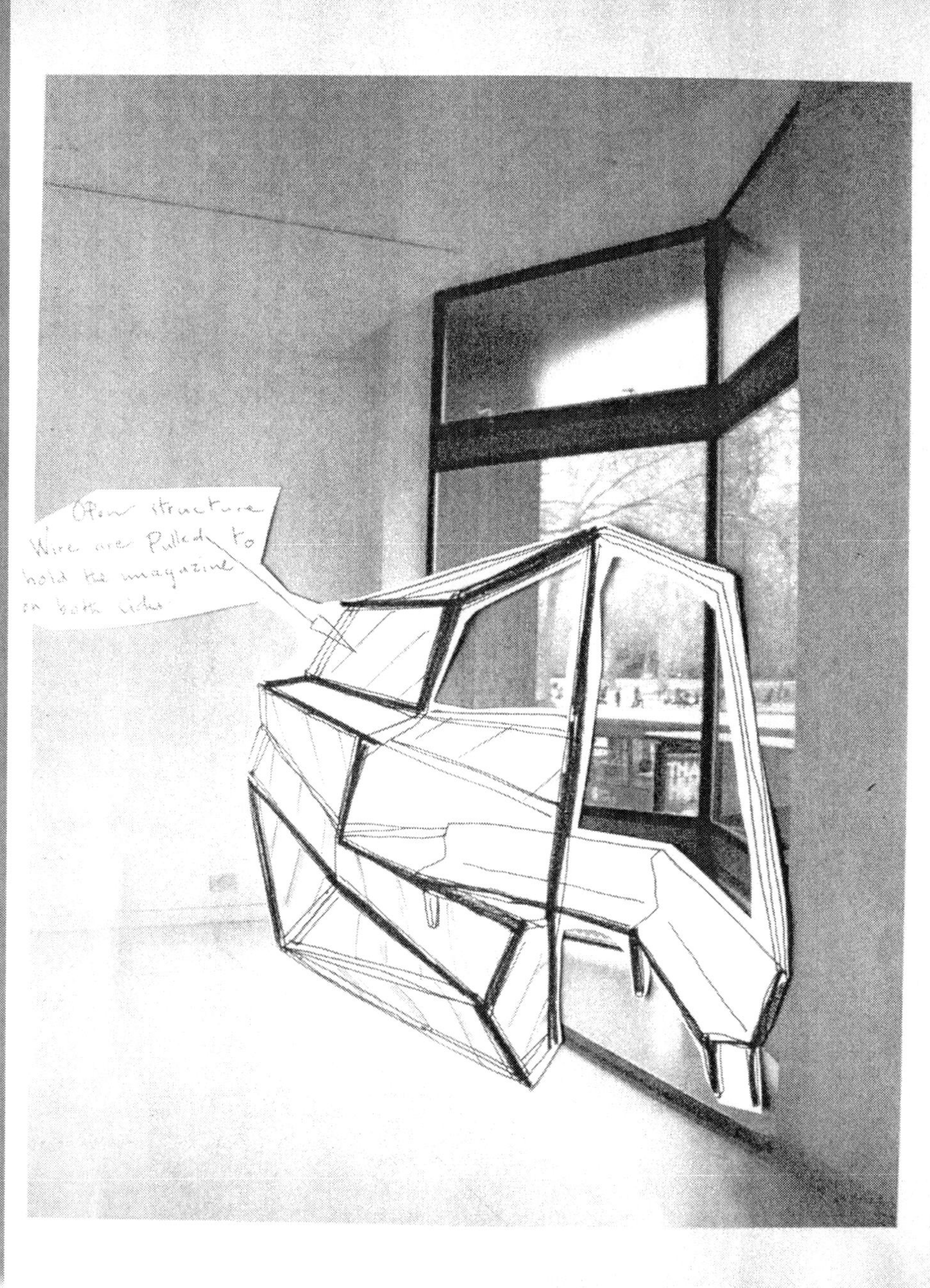

Open structure
Wire are Pulled to
hold the magazine
on both sides

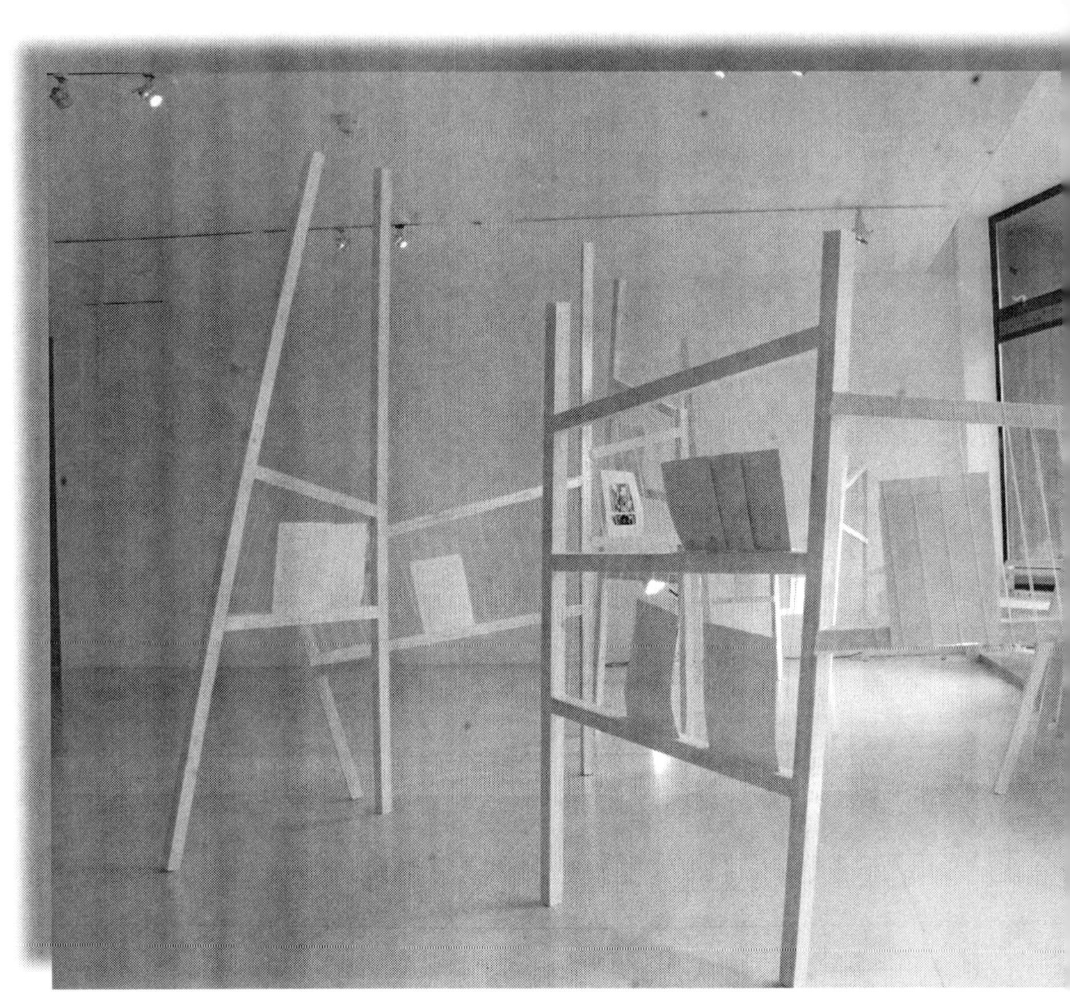

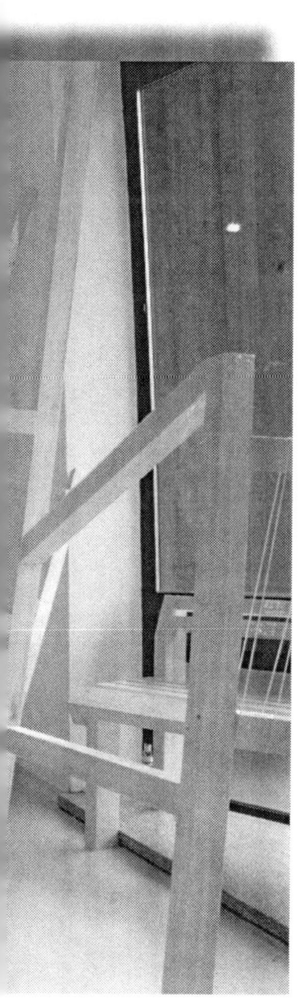

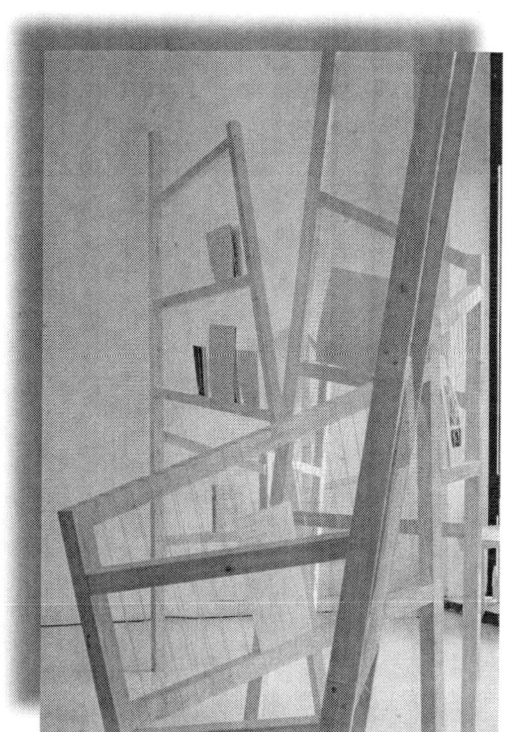

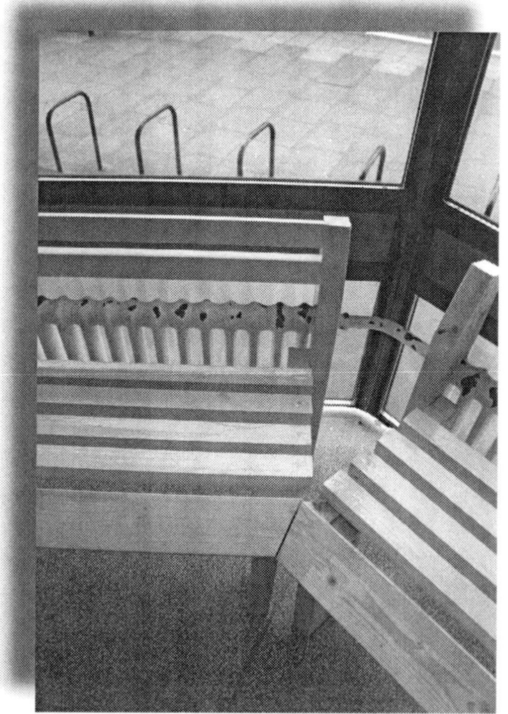

HETEROPIA

*We are not living in a neutral and white space. We are not
living, we are not dying, we are not living in the rectangle
of a white sheet of paper. We are living, we are dying,
we are loving in a square, cut, multi-coloured space, with
dark and light zones, differences of levels, steps stairs,
troughs, bumps, hard regions and some others that are
flakey, penetrable, porous. There are the passing regions,
the streets, the trains, the tubes. There are the open
regions of the transitional stop, the cafes, the cinemas,
the beaches, the hotels. And there are the closed regions
of time off and the home base.*

*I am dreaming of a science, and I say a science,
whose purpose would be these different spaces, these
'Other' places, these mythical and real contestations
of the space where we live. This science would not study
Utopias —— since the word must be reserved for what does
not have place at all — but would study the 'Heterotopias',
the spaces that are absolutely 'marginal', so obviously, this
science would be called, will be called, is already called,
the Heterotopology; the places that Society keeps out of
its borders, in the margins. These places are reserved for
people whose behaviour 'deviates' in comparison to the
average or conventional norm: nursing homes, psychiatric
wards, and of course, the prisons should also be added.
As should the 'rest-homes,' since after all, the idleness of
a society as busy as ours is perceived as a deflection, which
is actually a biological deflection when it is linked to old
age, and it is a constant deflection at least for all the ones
who do not have the discretion to die during the first three
weeks of their retirement.*

*Extract from 'Michel Foucault by himself'-1966-youtube
Translated from French by Clemence and Bahbak*

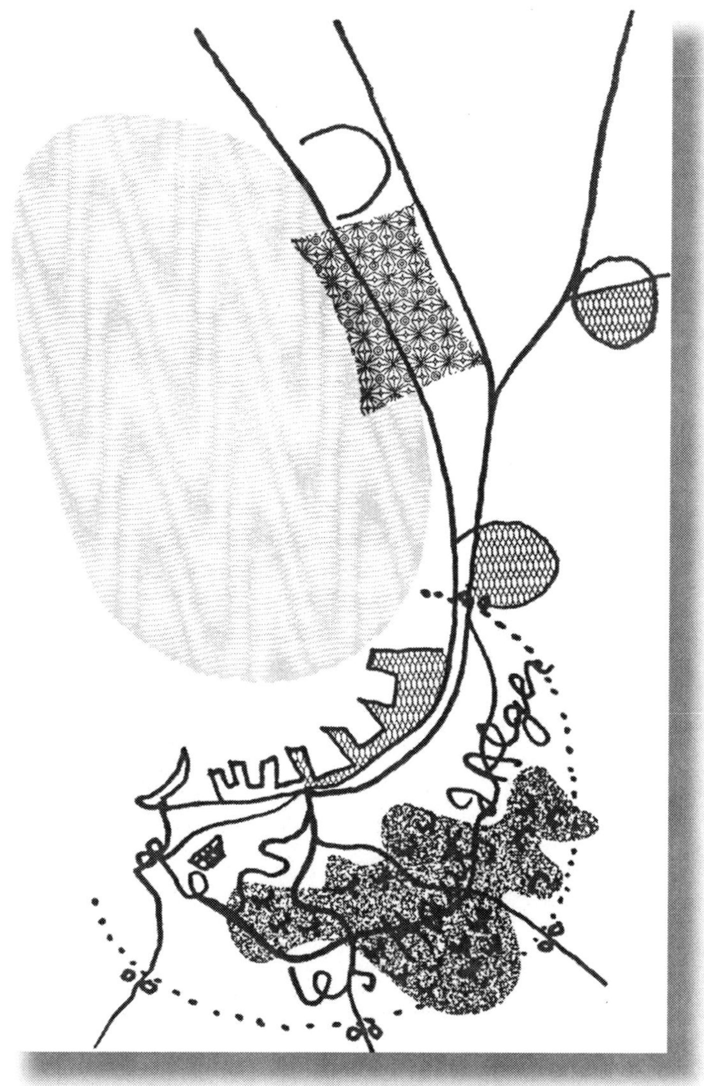

"Poesie sur Alger"
Le Corbusier

THE CUCKOO METHOD

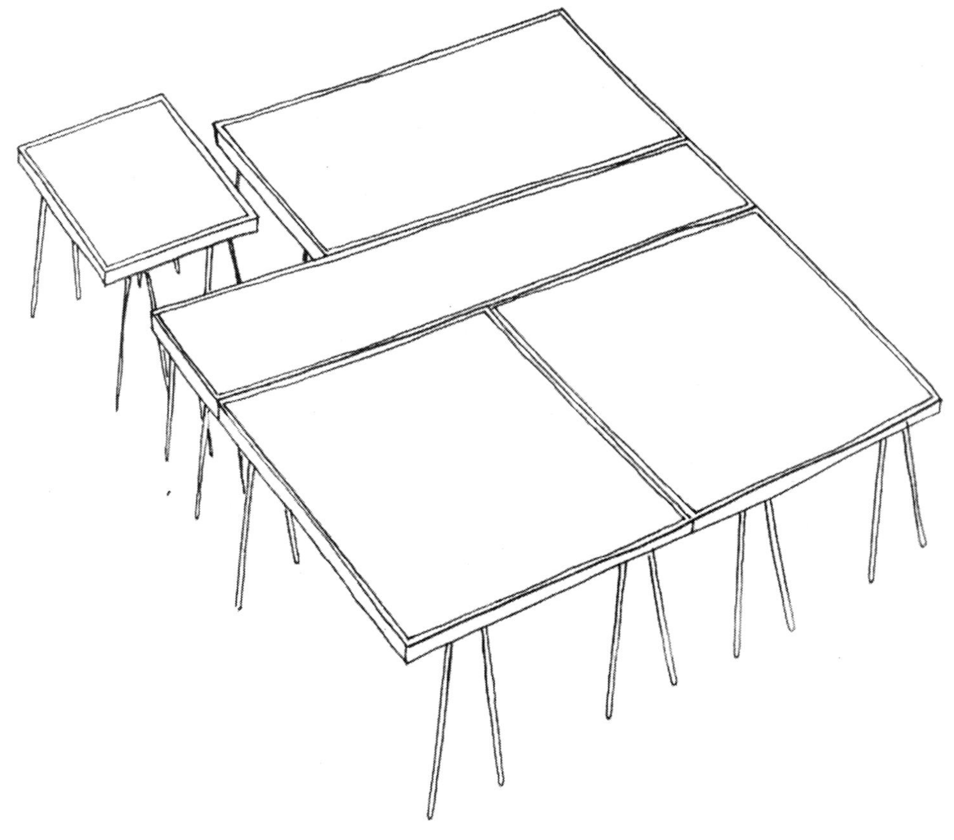

"The Cuckoo Method" is a program initiated by three students from Communication Art and Design. Each present themselves respectively as a graphic designer (Sarah Gottlieb), a film maker (George Wu) and an artist (Riitta Ikonen). It came as a partnership with two Product Design students, Fabien Cappello and myself.

There is the physical part that takes shape, as a pencil on paper, and a set of furniture for a mobile workshop studio. The objects do not relate to any one place. The structure keeps moving and taking place where the work is, where any given workshop is organized. It has to relate to the personal activity and needs of each member of the group; at the same time, these elements must be usable for workshop situations for 15 people.

This mobile situation explores non-place objects (there is no one workshop place, there is no one studio place) that must be renewed continuously for different scenarios. The flexibility of the set should also express a very precise and specific situation because no one workshop or working situation is the same. The immeasurable places, the different characters of the group, and the plural purpose of the set keep the guarantee of renewal without end.

It also makes sense to know about the genesis of the project, "The Cuckoo Method." in a school context, there are a lot of people who support the students, a lot of facilities that organize workshops and lectures, a lot of opportunities to meet people with different skills. This all ends suddenly after Graduation. Here is the most ambitious and generous point of the project: to try in some way to keep the huge energy going that the Royal College machine generates. It's an attempt to recreate the context of this *"highway" where knowledge is always passing and being caught by the alert ones. This is "The Cuckoo Method": to feed your own practice by those of others, as the Cuckoo bird does.*

May 2008

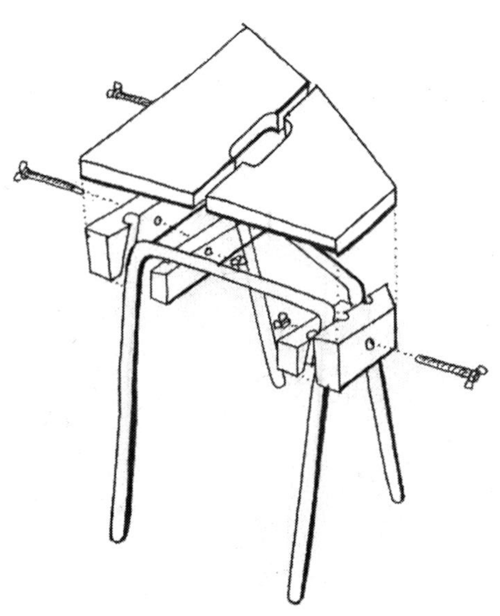

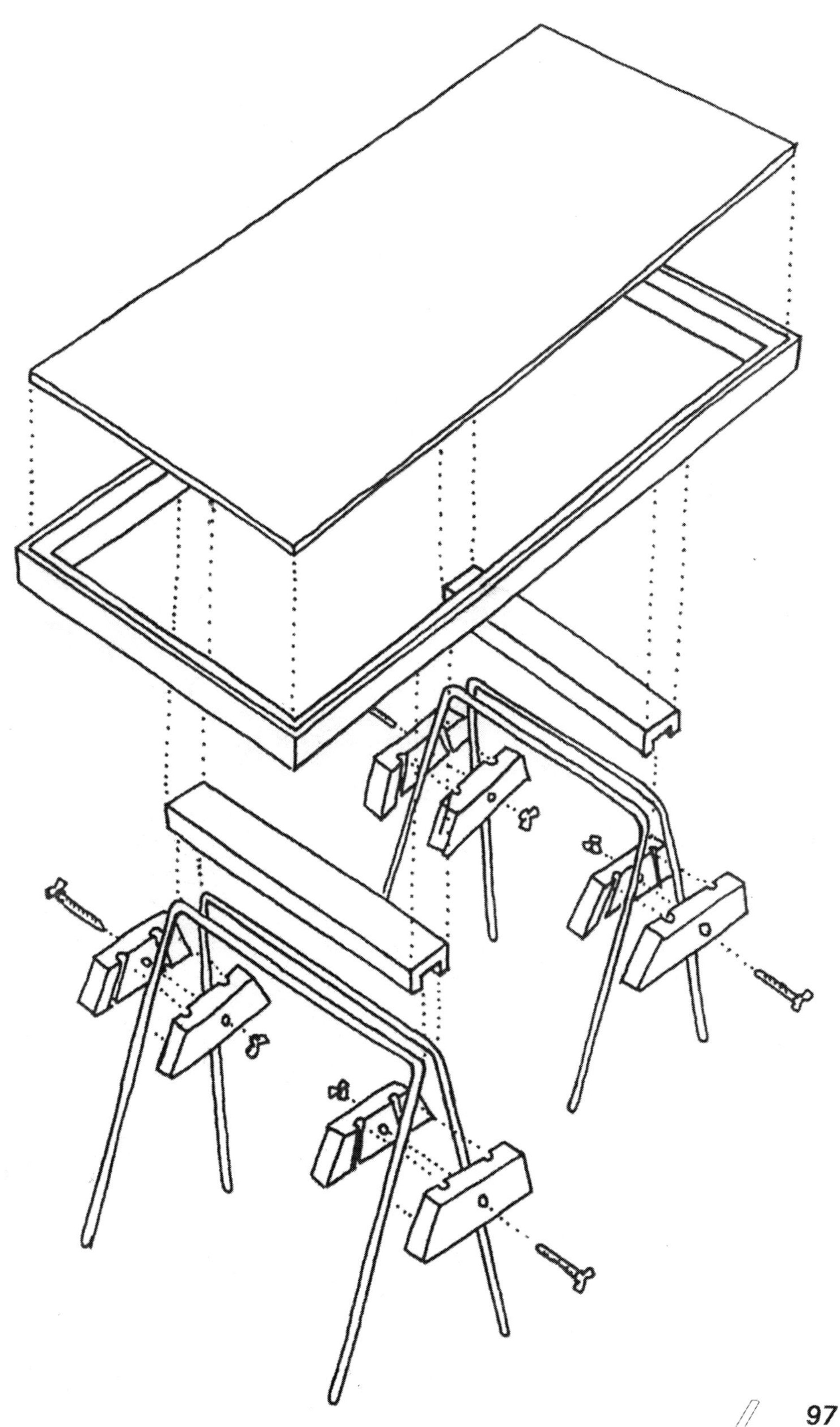

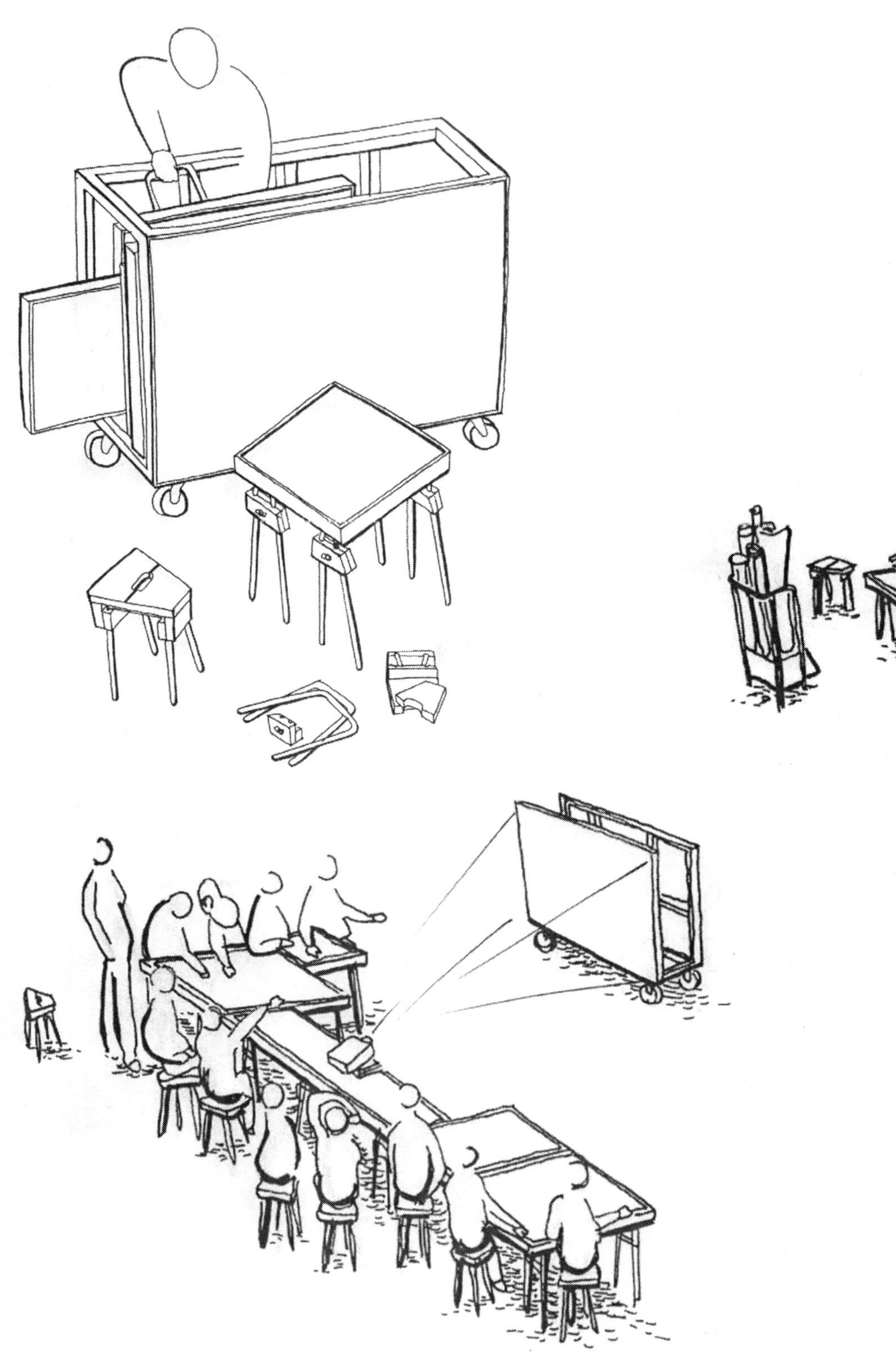

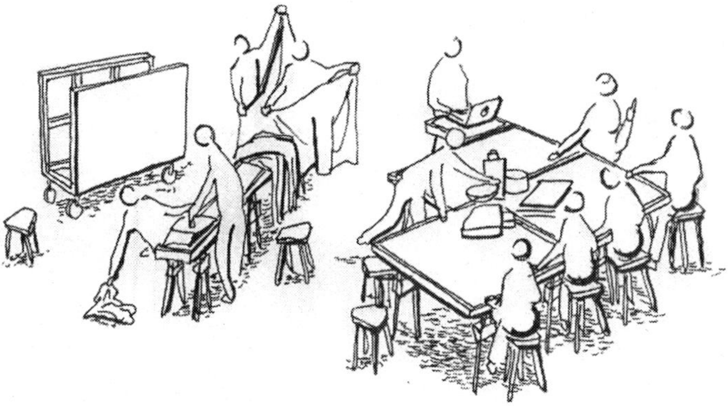

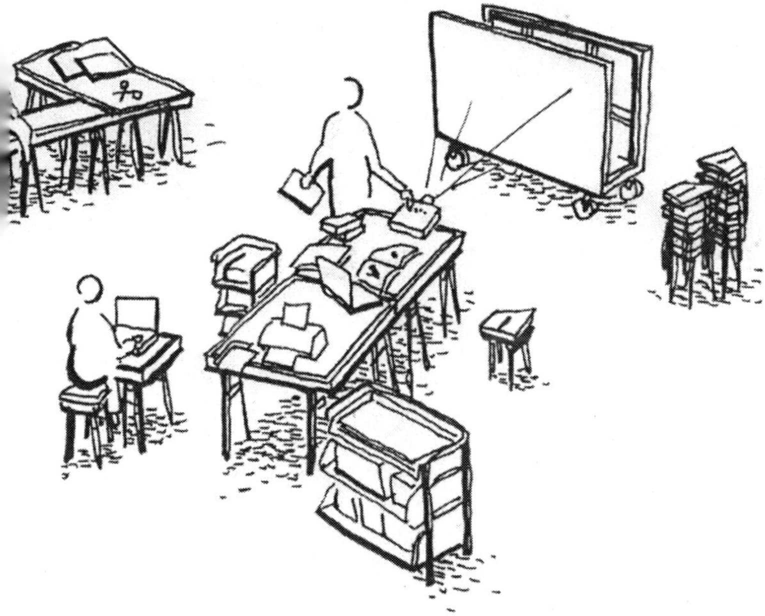